John Dick

A testimony to the doctrine, worship, discipline and government of the Church of Scotland

John Dick

A testimony to the doctrine, worship, discipline and government of the Church of Scotland

ISBN/EAN: 9783337274863

Printed in Europe, USA, Canada, Australia, Japan

Cover: Foto ©Lupo / pixelio.de

More available books at **www.hansebooks.com**

TESTIMONY

TO THE

Doctrine, Worſhip, Diſcipline, and Government of the Church of *SCOTLAND*,

AND THE

Covenanted work of Reformation

As it was Profeſſ'd in the Three Kingdoms:

TOGETHER WITH

An Account of the Perſecution of ſome of the moſt Eminent in Our Days, for their Adherence to the ſame.

As it was left in Write, by that truely Pious and Emmently, Faithfull and now Gorified Martyr ʲMr. *John Dick*.

To which is Added;

His Laſt Speech and Behaviour on the Scaffold, on the fifth day of *March* 1684. Which day he Sealed this Teſtimony, and left it to a particular Friend, to Communicate to the World after his Death; which was never Publiſhed till now, at the deſire of ſome reall and Sincere Lovers of the true Peace, and Welfare of the Church of *Scotland*.

Printed in the Year,

TESTIMONY

TO THE

Doctrine. Worship, Discipline and Goverament of the True *Presbyterian* Church of *Scotland*, and the Covenanted Work of *Reformation*, as it was profeſſed, in the Three Kingdoms.

By That Renowned, and now Glorified Martyr Mr. *John Dick*, who Suffered at *Ediuburgh* on the filth of *March* 1684.

Edinburgh 29 *Auguſt* 1683.

BEing called before Four of the Council; my Lord *Livingſton* (after Sir *William Paterſon* had Interrogat ſome few Queſtions, in the Outter-houſe, which becauſe confident with what follows, I omitt ,) ſays to me, Mr. *Dick*, There is a great Charge given in againſt you, which amounts to a great height ; what ſay you for your ſelf ? I anſwered, I crave you pardon, Sir, for you are a Stranger to me : One of them ſaid, it is my Lord *Livingſton* ; then I anſwered, I crave your Lordſhip would be more particular as to your Charge : Then he ſaid, That I was at *Pentland*, which I denied : Then he asked, where I had been ever ſince that time ? To which I anſwered, that being diſcovered to be a Converſer with ſome, that were there immediatly upon the back of the firſt Shot at the Biſhop, ſome Gentlemen being taken upon that Account, and threatned with the Boots, I was neceſſitat to leave the Nation. Then ſaid he, What ſay ye as to the Biſhop's Death, when he was killed? I told him, I thought he deſired an Account of my Principles, and I told him, I was a *Presbyterian*, and adhered to the Doctrine, Worſhip, Diſcipline, and Government of the Presbyterian Churches of the Three Nations, to which we were ſolemnly ſworn : He ſays, then you adhere to the Covenant : I anſwered, Yes, with my whole heart, and reſolves to do while I breath. Then, ſays the Biſhop of *Edinburgh*, do ye own the King's Authority ? I told him, my firſt Anſwer wherein I gave an Account of my Principles, was a ſufficient Anſwer for that : Some others ſtarted a Queſtion anent this, but the Biſhop anticipated my Anſwer, by ſaying, he ſpeaks very rationally according to his Principles, allowing the King as much as the Presbyterians do ; to which I added, conform to the Word of GOD. The Biſhop asked, if I acknowledged *Bothwell* to be Rebellion : I told him, I could not ſay it was, for I was confident the Generality of that people was not in Rebellion, being ſimply in ſelf Defence : the Biſhop asked, do ye own ſelf Defence lawful in any caſe cafe ? I faid yes in fome, Provoft *Ramfey* fayes (in what) to whom then I was offering to Anfwer; but I was Interrupted by the Bifhop of *Edinburgh*, who drew an argument from the effect accompanying the little Blood, that was fhed in Queen *Maries* Days, with what was fhed in the Inftine Wars: I Rejected his Argument, and albeit he Fathered the Effufion of Blood on the wrong fide of the Houfe, felf Defence being lawful by the word of God, by Laws of many Nations, and Law of Nature; I added let the World Judge, whither this Bifhop's Principles leads him right, that would have his fellow Subjects to hold up their Necks to Bloody Murderers, I fufpect he fhall be found a *Jefuite*, and thinks ftrange, that the Emperor of *Germany* fhould not fend for him, to preach this Doctrine to him.

Then asked one of them ftanding behind their Backs, if I Rode with Mr. *John Welfch* ? I faid, I knew not if I was bound to anfwer him, not knowing that he was a Member of the Council; well fayes one Sitting, what fay ye to it ? I Anfwered, yes I did, and I blefs God that ever I did fee him ; then fayes the ftander, do ye confefs ye Rode in Arms wth him, Riding in Arms ? I told him I had not Riden without Arms fince I was Seventeen or Eighteen years of Age : The Bifhop of *Edinburgh* fayes, I will propone a queftion to you, as a Clergy Man, I ftopped him there, and told him, I would Anfwer no queftion as a Clergy Man fitting there, at which fome others ftormed, he faid it was conform to my Principles, then the Bifhop preffed further his Argument from the effect in that abovementioned Comparifon. Provoft *Ramfey* faid you be newly taken, your Spirits aloft, its not time to reafon now, it will be more feafonable afterwards, upon which he defifted, the Bifhop asked, if I knew the Men, that were ftanding behind them ; which were *Hugh Stevenfon* and Mr. *Thomas Gordon*, who fhewed more Keennefs againft me, then the Bifhop himfelf, for which I forgive them, and I faid I knew all there, by Eye-fight, except my Lord *Livingfton* : The Bifhop asked when I knew him, I told when he was a Regent, in the College, but finding my felf in a miftake, I craved him pardon, telling him I was minding Commiffar *Wifheart*, but told that it was when he Preached in the Tron Church, that I knew him. He asked if ever I heard him there, I faid fometimes, in the Week days. He asked why not now ? I faid he was Lookt upon as an Honeft Man then, but had proved otherwife by *Breaking* his Oath to God, he faid he never took the Covenant, I faid that was a vain Defence. This is the Summe fo far as my Memory Serves.

Then, upon the laft day of Auguft 1683, being called before the Council, in prefence of the Lord Chancellor, Marquis of *Dowglas*, the Earl of *Tweddell*, Bifhop of *Edinburgh*, Prefident of the Seffion, *Colington*, *Caftlehill*, *Abbotfhall*, after the Chancellor had conferred with me, a confiderable time, the Clerk having cleared fuch of my Affertions, as they judged fit to make ufe of againft me, they defired me to Subfcribe the fame, which I refufed to do till it were rectified, they having fome things in it, wrong; and others, mifplaced. At laft this Meeting Refulted in this, that I fhould Subfcribe the following, Declaration? both before the Council and Jufticiary

Mr. *John Dick*, Son David Dick Writer in *Edinburgh*, being called and Examined, in prefence of the faid Lords, declares ; He owns the work of Reformation,

mation, as the fame is contained, in the Confeffion of Faith and Catechifms, conform to the Covenant againft Popery, Prelacy, Erastianifme, &c. And is refolved, by the Lords Strength, to abide in the fame.

Declares, that as to *Epifcopacy*, and Laws Eftablifhing the fame, he cannot underftand it, to be Lawful; becaufe, fince the Kings Reftoration, there has been no free nor Lawful Parliaments, and he thinks by reafon, albeit the Members thereof were Elected, in the ordinary way; Yet when the Members Meet, there was unlawful Oaths impofed upon them, and there upon, feverals of them left the Parliament, and fo he underftands, that it is not a free nor lawful Parliament, and thinks, that *Epifcopacy* and *Erastianifme* is eftablifhed in that and fubfequently Parliaments were contrary to the Word of God, and that the *Supremacy* herein eftablifhed is moft horrid Blafphemy. I added here to the Chancellor, that I hoped, his Lordfhip would not be offended at this, feeing he had fworn the fame, in the Teft; but they refufed to write this, in my fubfcribed Declaration: Being Interrogate, if he owned the Proclamation and Declarationat *Sanquhair* and *Hamiltoun*, Declares, he does not own the *Sanquhair* Declaration, as being inconfiftent with his Principles, fuch as the cutting off of the wicked; and having himfelf read the *Hamiltoun* Declaration, Declares, he owns the fame, and that, when they were finvaded and affaulted, by any Perfons whatfoever, in their Exercifes of Reformed Religion and Worfhip, they were obliged to ftand to their own Defence, and owns the Lawfullnefs of Field Conventicles, and their being in Arms to Defend themfelves in cafe of being Molefted; And he himfelf was ever ready to own and defend his Brethren in Arms, when invaded for Religion; And declares, that the Invafion made againft them at *Pentland*, and *Bothwell*, they being in the Exercife of his Religion, was Service done to the Devil, and Refiftance made by them, was Service done to GOD.

Confeffes, that before *Bothwell* Bridge he had riden in Arms with Mr. *Welfch* through the Countrey, and bleffes God for it; Confeffes, he was at a Meeting at *Lefmehago* before *Bothwell*, when Lieutenant *Dalziel* with a Party came upon them, and was one of thefe, that engaged againft that Party.

Denies, he was fat *Drumclogg*; But confeffes, he was at *Bothwell*, and thinks, that Mr. *John Welfch* ftayed about half a year in the Countrey thereafter, but he was only, about eight days in Company with him after *Bothwell*, in this Kingdom: Confeffes, the King is lawful King Born, and came Lawfully to the Crowns of thefe Kingdoms, and that he is lawful King of this Kingdom, and owns the Kings Authority, conform to the Word of GOD, that is to fay, That he is impowered to Govern for GOD's Glory and the good of his People, and to be a Terror to evil doers, and encourager to well; and Declares, that the Act of Supremacy, as it is explained by the Act of Parliament; that the turning out of Presbyterian Intereft, and overturning the Work of Reformation, moft unlawful Acts, and being exprefly contrary to the Word of God, can not be Binding upon the Declarent; and that Covenants are binding upon the Nations, and fhall be fo, while Sun and Moon endures; and that that Oath, called the *Teft*, is a moft unlawful and horrid Oath, and he is not obliged to take the fame.

He Declares, As to killing the Archbishop of St. *Andrews*, he cannot give Judgment anent it, it not being an Act of his own; but that some of these, that were called the Actors, whom he knew (and particularly one *William Dingwal*) were Godly and Just Men.   *sic subscribitur,* · *John Dick*.

The last Day of *August* 1683, There being many Noblemen in the Court, which day Mr. *John Dick* being present, was Examined, in presence of the Justices then sitting in Judgment, and the abovewritten Confession emitted by him in presence of the Council, being read, he acknowledged the same, and every particular of the same in presence of the said Justices. *Sic subscribitur,* *John Dick, Maitland, James Fowls, John Lockhart, Alexander Seton.*

Upon *September* 4, 1683, I Mr. *John Dick*, Son to *David Dick* Writer in *Edinburgh*, being Called before the Lords of Justiciary being then present; it was demanded, if I had any thing to say for my self? I answered, Yes, my Lord, I have somewhat to add to my Lyble; they asked, what was that? then I proceeded as follows: I Mr. *John Dick* Prisoner, in Name and by the Appointment of Our Blessed Lord and Master Jesus Christ, Declare, That the Blood of all the Presbyterians, that have been Executed for their Principles, is horrid Murder; by whatsomever Law they have been judged; and that in the Person of every Individual one, who have suffered simply on this Account, Our Blessed Lord Jesus Christ, hath been as really crucified, as He was by *Pilate* and the *Jews* at *Jerusalem*. And this I desire may be holden as a part of my former Declaration and Confession, emitted before the Council and Justices. This I called for, and subscribed, blessing the Lord that had given me a hand so to do. They refused to add it to my Declaration, judging they had too much already. I required all that were present Witnesses, that I had declared the same, and Appealled them all to Christ's Bar at the Great Day, to Answer for what they had done, and were doing. They asked if I would have an Advocat? I said, My Lords, that is ordinarly denied to Persons in my condition: they declared, I should have as many as I pleased; I said, I would have none, but my Blessed Lord Jesus Christ, Blessed be His Holy Name for it, He is both with me, and in me. The Justice Clerk asked, if I was a Quaker, or a *Fifth Monarchry* Man? I told him, I abhorred both, yet my Affection was relevant, being Blessed of my God with the Grace of Faith: And then they read my Indictment, and asked at every Article, to which I answered affirmatively.

Then, did the Justice Clerk ask, if I had any thing to say for my self, I said, I Blessed the Lord I had: they Desired me to proceed, Answer, I expect my Lords, being a Free Born *Scots* Man, I shall have the Priviledge allowed me, that the Christians in former days had among the Heathens, the Justice Clerk bids me proceed there are two things, which I hope your Lordship will grant e're we proceed, further, first do you not Acknowledge, that the Almighty God *Jehovah* is Supream Lord & Governour of Heaven and Earth, & that all Kings in the Earth, are but his Deputs & Servants; the Justice Clerk sayes yes. The Second, Do ye not Acknowledge, that all the Law in the World among Christians must Strike Sail to the great Law, the Law of God: to which I got no Answer; whereupon I took Witnesses and Protested, that it might be Recorded in Heaven; then they press'd me to proceed. I told him the Advocat (offering to follow his own method) had drawn out my Declaration : my

Lords

fords you have been at much pains to seek my Accusation, I have been so Ingenuous to Exhibite it to you my self, for which I Bless the Lord, first Article that I own my self to a Presbyterian, and to be bound to continue so, conform to a Covenant, that can not be Infringed by no Power under Heaven

Now, my Lords, I being under such strong Impressions of those my Obligations, the least I can expect, is to know by what Authority this is broken ? To this I got no Answer, they declined further Questioning, causing and commanding the Jury to be called, and after they had asked, if I had any thing to say against them, they swore them; desiring me, that if I had any thing to say to the Jury, to proceed: I said, my Lords, its hard to devolve me upon a Jury before I be heard, for which I charge you all to make ready to Answer before my Great Master, at the Great Day, and this Jurie also, as to what ye do in this Affair. Then they desired me to speak to the Jury, for the Advocat was to have the last word : then I thinking I should have occasion to have Reasoned with the Advocat anent my Lybll, told the Jury, That the Principle I held in my Declaration, was of such a Nature, as I durst not, if I had as many Lives as there are Pickles of Sand on the Sea Shoar to redeem them all, with the quitting of the least hair-breadth thereof: Then I pressed the Obligation of the Covenant, expecting the Advocat's Answer. They asked if I had done ? I answered, Yes, as to this. Then the Advocat began his Course, wherein he did little more than Repeat my Declaration, without offering any thing against any Article therein, except against that of Defensive Arms, his Defence against which, was this, that he had read of Defensive Arms betwixt two single Men; But for multitudes, he knew no Defensive Arms against standing Laws: Then did I offer to Reply; but they would not suffer me, but recommended me to the Jury, strictly Tying them that the Condemners should put it to after their Name and Assizers likewise: Then I came conveyed to the Outter-House by the Guard, where my Father came to me within a little, and told me he had been dealing with the Lords for a Delay, but had not got it so long as he expected: I told him, that whatever my good Lord's will was, I was satisfied, but I'le speak nothing of that my self: He says well, I knew that, and so he leaves me.

I am called in again within half an Hour, and my Sentence intimated to be Hanged at the Grass-Mercat, upon the 26th instant. I said my Lords without a Hearing, either before the Justices or Jurors, this Practice was never parallel'd among Heathens, and further my Lords and Jurors; I declare, and that upon good grounds, that if upon this Sentence you Hang me, you shall not be innocent of Crucifying the Lord afresh, in me his poor and insignificant Member: They called, suffer him to speak no more. This is the sume, so far as my brittle Memory will allow, and I am confident there wants little or nothing of Moment: Now for satisfaction, both to Friends and Foes, I have Judged it my Duty to add what follows.

My blessed Lord and Master hath determined mine Heart, in all this my my Tryal (next to his own Glory) to have my Eye upon the Edification, and Confirmation of his poor Distrest and Opprest People, my Companions in Tribulation, as also to design as much as possible the Conviction of hs, and our profest and avowed Enemies; moved me, without any previous Deliberation,

to

to affert thefe Principles and practices contained in my Indictment, and to add that other affertion which I did before my Sentence, before the Juftices and Affize: I fay my bleffed Lord having thus determined and moved me (for which I blefs his Name) has not left me in the Dark, as to Grounds and Warrants for what in and through fuch a poor and empty Reed, as I am he hath done, which Grounds while I offered to the Juftices and Affizes, for my Vindication, I am (contrare to all Law, Equity and Reafon) refufed that Privilege, a Privilege granted even by the Heathens: Thefe Grounds, I have thought fit to leave under my Hand, for the comfort of the Lords People, and (if not the conviction) the Terror of his (and ours for his fake) Proud, infolent Enemies as follows.

You Remember, that before I offered any Defence, I Demanded of the Juftices, that they would grant me the thefe two Principles, to wit. Firft, that the Almighty God *Jehovah*, was Supreame Lord and Mafter, over all in Heaven, and in Earth, and that all Kings, and other Rulers in the Earth, are his Deputes and Servants; this they granted. The fecond is, that all Laws in the Earth muft ftrike-Sail, and Vail their Caps to the Supream Law, *the Word of God*, and be Regulate by it, this they refufe to grant, which I lookt upon as moft Horrid Blafphemy, and took Inftruments on the Refufal thereof, (which I know ftands Recorded in Heaven, to be produced againft the Denyers, at the Great Day of the Lord) I doubt not, if that Young Noble Man who Refufed me this, had been prefent, when Mr. *John Paterfon* Propofed the Queftion to me, if our King was Comptable to any, to whom I Anfwered, he was: He asked to whom, I faid to thefe, by whom he was Intrufted: He Anfwered, then he could not be Soveraign, Intimating that there could be no Soveraign but one, whom we *Presbyterians* hold to be the Almighty God *Jehovah*; to whom alone indeed it is high Treafon, for any Mortall to fay what doeft thou : It being lawful *de jure*, to ask any Mortall King an Account of his doings, as need Requires; though *de facto* in the cafe of Cruel Tyrany, this be Dangerous : I fay, if this Noble Man had heard this, he had not fo rafhly Refufed my Affertion ; But whatever our Rulers do, I do, and I hope with me, all that has the leaft Smattering of Religion will both grant, and firmly in his ftrength, hold both thefe Principles; for to me to grant the former, and refufe the Latter, implys a Contradiction : now laying thefe for two fure and inviolable Foundations : I go on, as if I were before the Juftices and Jury, to deliver my own grounds, which my God laid to my Hand, and anfwer any thing of Objections, I meet with either before the Secret Council or Juftices.

Now my Lords of Jufticary, and you Jurers (taken thefe Principles for granted) my firft Affertion I have to Vindicate, is this; that I own the work of Reformation, as the fame is contained in the Confefion of Faith and Catechifms, conform to the Covenant againft *Popery*, *Prelacy* and *Eraftianifme*, and am Refolved by the Lords Strength, to bide by the fame, (and feing, that it is Lawful for any Man to Weild his Arms, for his beft Advantage) to this I Subjoin the Inviolable Obligation of the Covenant, to adhere to thefe Principles and Practices. Now my Lords this work of Reformation, thefe Principles and Practices being fuch, as I find Warranted from the practice of Chrift, and hi

Apoſtles, and not only I, but his Majeſty, and all, under him, in theſe Nations, being by the Oath of God, which ſhall never be Diſolved by any Humane Power the leaſt I can expect of your Lordſhips is, that ye will offer ſome what, that may be Satisfactory to my Conſcience, in this point, if ye deny me this, then ſhall the World judge that ye will Murder me, becauſe ye will Murder me, all that I have heard from any of your Members againſt my Principles, ſimply was from the Biſhop of *Edinburgh*, who after he had inſinuate an Argument with me in Doctrine and Worſhip, ſeemed fairly to inſinuate, that Diſcipline and Government were left undetermined, my anſwer to this is, that this is horrid Blaſphemy, and no leſs uopn the whole Matter then to ſay, that our bleſſed lord Jeſus Chriſt was leſs faithful in the Houſe of God than was *Myſes*, and who having the leaſt Senſe of a Deity dares to averre this ? Well my Lords this being all I have offered by any of your Lordſhips againſt my Principles, I hope it ſtands firmly rooted in the Hearts of all that love our Lord Jeſus Chriſt, that they are thereby not in the leaſt ſhaken and ſince it is ſo, which I muſt take for granted , having nothing offered to the contrary : I muſt for the confirmation of the ſecond brench of this aſſertion poſe your Lordſhs, by what Authority an Oath, a ſolemn Oath made betwixt the living GOD's Party contracter-on the one hand, and his Majeſty and the whole Body of theſe Nations on the other hand, in as ſolemn a manner as ever Covenant was tranſacted I ſay, I muſt ask by what Authority this Covenant is infringed and broken ? To this I get no anſwer neither except what I got from the above mentioned Biſhop, who told me he had not taken this Covenant : For anſwer, it had been a great pity this maſter Prelate of yours, had not been amongſt the People of Iſrael at that time, when the Plague of GOD overtook them for the breach of Covenant made, as ſome thinks, Four hundred years before that with the Gibeonites, and this Covenant in it ſelf nothing ſo juſtiſiable as this which may Bleſſed Lord has ſet me here to Juſtifie; I ſay, it had been a pity, this Pitifull Prelate had not been there, its not likely he had obtained a Suſpenſion of this Famine upon this head ; but let this proud Prelate conſider, that he Charges the Almighty with injuſtice in this Practice, which you have Recorded in the 2 *Sam*. 21. *Chap*. He muſt either own this a piece of Horrid Blaſphemy, or elſe conſeſs his Argument is of no force: Now having I hope, Rolled out of the way any thing I have offered for my Satisfaction in this matter, to come nearer the point, I charge your Lordſhips or any here who ſets themſelves againſt me on theſe heads again to tell me, by what Authority this Oath binding to two Neceſſary and Indiſpenſible Duties is repelled ? Dare any Mortall here hold up his Face to Heaven, and averr that his Majeſtey's Acts Reſciſſory does repell it, then let him do it upon his Peril, and when he has done, know that beſides his Blaſphemy in it, he Contradicts the firſt Principle, which your Lordſhips have granted me. That this may be the clearer, I hope all will grant that none can Diſſolve an Oath made by another, except he be above that other in power and Authority of ſuch a Decree as gives Right to do it, of this I Remember, only two Inſtances in Scripture. The one is, That of a Husband if he hear his Wife making a Vow, if he be not Satisfied with it, he may then unty it ; But if by his Silence he let it paſs, the Oath ſtands firm. The Seconds is of a

Father

Father having a Daughter in the Family, to whom it is granted to annull the Oath he heares her making while in his Family, and when out of the Family, the power ceafes: From this it is evident, that this is a Superiority over them, that Intitles them to this Privilege. Since it is fo, dare any without Horror, offer once of Dreaming to apply this in our cafe? I fufpeck by this time the Juftice Clerk finds himfelf outfhot, in granting my firft Principal; O that the Lord would open their Eyes, to fee the Affronted Indignities done to our moft Glorious God, in thefe their moft horrid and Abominable Practices. Now having Removed what is offered by the Oppofers, and fettled by undenyed Arguments, my Affertion of the equity of our Work of Reformation, and the Inviolable Obligation of the Covenant, while Sun and Moon endures to own the fame; I hope I fhall not need to rack my Judgement, for Arguments to prove; that my Devolvement on an Affize without a hearing,(after I had offered to Juftifie my Principles and Practices from the word of God) is not only a denying of thefe my two Principles, but the moft horrid of Murders, as I hope fhall be cleared more fully in the clofe, and here you may fee the reafon of denying my fecond Principle, but of this more afterwards.

The fecond Affertion I am to defend is, that the Laws overturning the *Presbyterian* Church & Eftablifhing *Epifcopacy*, particularly thefe three Acts. To wit firft, The Act Refciffory, whereby at one dafh the Glorious Fabrick, fometime the Glory of thefe Nations is Overturned. Secondly, The Act of Supremacy, and Act Explanatory of the fame, whereby our Bleffed Lord is fet by his Chair, and a poor Worm fet down in his Room. Thirdly, That Act called the *Teft*, a Hotchpotch of Nonfenfe Lies and Contradictions; that thefe and others of their nature were null, and afferted Principally; becaufe contrary to exprefs Texts of Scripture (and this poffibly has Straitened my Antagonifts, as to the granting of our Bleffed Lords word, to be the Supream Law,) and for Confirmation of this, I afferted, I thought the Parliament enacting thefe Acts was alfo null, as not being free, a Qualification abfolutly requifite in all Parliaments in this Nation, the Privileges of which I am bound by the Covenant made with the Almighty God to affert. Now my Lords, and you Affizers, I take forgranted, that all Laws of Men contrary to exprefs Texts of Scripture are null, and that thefe Acts, and all of that nature are fuch; I fhall in the Lords ftrength endeavour to prove. And Firft, the whole work of Reformation being agreeable to the Word of God, and though it were not foin it felf, (as I am firmly perfwaded it is) yet in my cafe, by all Men who have not with their Confcience, Debauched away their reafon alfo, it muft be granted to be; (feing I have had nothing offered to the contrary) and I being under the Oath of God to maintain, Propagate and Defend the fame; the Acts overturning the fame exprefly, Contradicts not only all thefe Scriptures, upon which it is founded (which time will not allow me to Enumerate here) and you may find in your Confeffion of Faith, Noted upon the Margine of that Book, but alfo the Third Command, *Thou fhalt not take the Name of the Lord thy God in vain*; and that, perform thy Vows unto the Lord with multitudes of this Nature, which upon a very moderate inquiry may eafily be found. Now my Lords, if my Second Principle be found, as I hope your Lordfhips are perfwaded it is, for all you have faid to the contrary, I hope your Lord-

fhips

ſhips will find your ſelves concerned to ſatisſie me as to theſe, e're you proceed to the Execution of this your Unparalleled Sentence. As to the Second, I think I ſhall need to be at leſs pains about it, in reſpect, not only your Lordſhips; But I ſuſpect the greater part, if not all the Aſſizers have Sworn as to the ſame in your *Teſt*, That it is Blaſphemy for Man or Angel, to preſume to Intrude into the headſhip of the Church, as being only peculiar, to my Bleſſed Lord and Maſter Jeſus Chriſt.

But for Confirmation, I deſire you to conſider theſe Scriptures, *Firſt*, the firſt Chapter of the *Epheſians* 22. 23. *Verſes, And he hath put all things under his Feet, and gave him to be the Head over all things to the Church, which is his Body the fullneſs of him that filleth all in all. Iſa. 9. Chapter 6, 7. Verſes.* And the Second *Pſalm*, Now that any Law made againſt theſe expreſs Scriptures is null, with the conſideration foreſaid, of your own Confeſſion, and the Conſent of the greater part, if not the whole (ſo far as I know) Reformed Churches, would ſeem to be ſufficiently warranted.

The Third. As to that of the Teſt, that it is null will eaſily appear at the firſt reading thereof, to any that will be ſo daring, as to aver, that to ſwear Nonſence and Contradictions is no Sin : That it is Nonſence to ſwear to defend the Proteſtant Religion againſt Presbyterians, and a Contradiction too, I muſt aſſert ; ay and while you condeſcend upon a Proteſtant Church who have expunged us out of their Number, except that Abominable, Perjured Prelatical Party, whom I cannot, nor (I truſt in GOD) ever ſhall own for any other thing, than Emiſſaries from Hell, ſent through *Rome*, for the Confounding of the Chriſtian World : And if to ſwear the King to be Head of the Church and with the ſame Breath, that is horrid Blaſphemy, ſo to do, if it be not a Contradiction, I know not what is. For confirmation hereof, Let the Unfreeneſs of the Parliaments be conſidered, and I hope none who love our Lord Jeſus Chriſt, will doubt, that I had good ground to aſſert, what I have through His Grace aſſerted ; and I bleſs His Name thereof I am no ways aſhamed. And if the Enemies will, ſure I am, they muſt grant, that they were all bound in Conſcience, Law, Equity and Reaſon, to have told ſo much, which they, nor none of them, had the Confidence to do. The Application I leave to the Impartial Reader.

The Third thing I have in task, is to defend theſe Aſſertions following, to wit, That I own the *Hamiltoun* Declaration, and when we were invaded or Aſſaulted by any perſon whatſoevr, in the Exerciſe of our Reformed Religion and Worſhip upon that account, we were obliged to ſtand to our own Defence : That I own the Lawfulneſs of *Field-Conventicles*, and our being in Arms to defend our ſelves in caſe of being Moleſted ; and that I my ſelf was ever ready to Own and Defend my Brethren in Arms when invaded as ſaid is. And declaring that the Invaſions made againſt the Lord's people at *Pentland* and *Bothwell*, they being then in the Exerciſe of their Religion, was ſervice done to the Devil, and the reſiſtance made by them in their own Defence was Service done to GOD. Now the ſume of all theſe Aſſertions is, that it is the Duty of Proteſtant Reformed Churches to ſtand to the Defence of their Reformation and Religion : Eſpecially with this conſideration, that with their Religion they are alſo aſſaulted as to their Privileges, as in the freedom of

Parliaments

Parliaments, and many other paarticulars which if time would allow I could enumerate ; Confidering efpecially, That this Church and Kingdom are obliged fo to do, by a moft folemn Oath made to the ever living GOD, they their Kings their Princes and Nobles, and the whole Body of the Realm, and that this Oath ftands ftill unviolate as you may fee above. The cafe thus ftated, I hope our Adverfaries will not deny, that if the Turk, or any Foreign Enemy, fhould invade us, and in his Declaration fhew, That he would not lay down his Arms, till we fhould Renounce our Reformed Religion, and quite with all our Civil Priviledges ; I hope none, in his Right Wits, will refufe, that it were our Duty, Man and Mother-Son, from the higheft to the loweft , to draw to Arms in our own Self-defence. But it is like fome will fay, That though we were bound fo to do againft Foreigners, yet we may not do fo againft our Lawful Princes. To this I Anfwer, Firft, They are divided among themfelves here ; Some granting, that in fome cafes, even their own Lawful Princes may be refifted, and the Arms of Innocent Self-defence made ufe of againft them. Others fay, No! But whatever they fay or think, either this Pofition fhall ftand to the World's End, That there was never a Power given of God, to any Mortal, to rugg and deftroy the Souls of the Subjects, and to ruine them in their Civil Interefts ; or otherways, there was never a Power given of GOD to any Mortal, to enact iniquity by a Law, and to force Obedience to thefe iniquious Laws by Fire and Sword, as it is in our cafe; And if any Monarch or any pretending Commiffion from him, fhould arrogate a Power to do fo, the Subject beyond all contraverfie is called to ftand to his own Defence, and vindicate the honour of his Great Supream Mafter, feeing he is violented to the Denyal of Alledgeance to him, by his pretended Depute or Servant : I fuppofe this will not be refufed by any that believes that there is a GOD. And for my felf, I think he who comes out with Armed force to compel me to fin, fhould be in the felf fame way ferved, as he who fhould with Violence come to drive me quick into Hell, and I fuppofe the greateft of the pretended Loyalifts amongft us if they heard and believed the Screichings of the Damned Souls there, and faw no other way of efcaping, but either over or through their Soveraign, they would venture upon either, rather than be driven into it. And to fay any Soveraign how Lawful fo ever, otherwife has fuch a power is to contradict that Scripture, *Kings are given to be a Terror to evil doers, and encouragers of well doers.* If it be faid thefe things fhould be in a civil manner Reprefented or Arms be taken : I fhall readily grant this, but why were thefe Minifters and Gentlemen taken and incarcerate who were endeavouring thus ? And why was there an Act of Parliament, if I may call it fo, made Dicharging any of the Subjects to meet and Confult in order to this? And indeed I think he fhould be extruded the Society of Mankind who would make this affertion, that our otherwife Lawful Prince may lawfully do any of thefe things abovementioned to his Subjects, and that the World may fee, I fpeak not here at random, be pleafed to confider thefe two Scriptures, Firft the 14 *Chap.* of the firft Book of *Samuel.* Secondly the 12 *chapter* of the firft Book of the *Kings.* To this I add the 20 *Chap.* of the fecond Book of the *Chron.* 16. *verfe,* Now whofoever fhall ponder and ferioufly confider thefe three places, will find three Kings of the Lawfulnefs of whofe coming to their Crowns I know none

that

that doubt, all three refifted by their Subjects, the firft in offering to perform a rafh and finful Oath, the fecond for offering finfully to opprefs his people; The third for dipping too far in the Matters of God, for which he had no Commiffion.

Now, with Submiffion to the more Judicious, I humbly conceive the Ground of the Equity of this Refiftance lyes here: That Kings and Subjects are under a Twofold Relation one to another; Firft, in refpect of the Almighty GOD, who is the Only Abfolute Sovereign and Great Lord, both he and they are Fellow-Subjects; and with him, in finning againft the Laws of This Our Great Mafter, none of his Fellow-Subjects dare, under the pain of Eternal Damnation, in the leaft fymbolize; but on the contrary, adhering to our Allegiance to Our Great Liege Lord, we are bound by Our Allegiance, in our Stations, to refift every thing offered to His Difhonour, by whomfoever. I hope this Truth is clear to any that knows, that the Laws of GOD are equally binding upon Kings and Subjects. The fecond Relation is, That whereby the King, under GOD, is King, and to Rule the People for GOD's Glory, and the Good of the Kingdom, and to be a Terror to Evil Doers, and an Encourager to Well Doers; in which Relation the People are his Subjects. Now, there is none of my Perfwafion, but are willing *to give Cæfar his due*, that is, to obey all his Lawfull Commands, and yeild him all Encouragement imaginable, he Ruling in the Fear of GOD, the People for GOD's Glory, and his and their own Good. But if a King, fhaking off all Fear of GOD, will enter in Open Hoftility againft Heaven, and force his People, by Open Hoftility, to fhare with him in thefe Abominations; I again fay, the People are obliged, in purfuance of their Allegiance to their Supream Lord, not only to refufe Obedience to this His Depute, but alfo to refift him in purfuance of this his War againft the Great LORD. I hope, I fhall need to fay nothing for clearing of this, to any that knows that there is a GOD, whofe Holy Nature entitles Him to Abfolute Sovereignty, and to Whom Subjection is due from that His Bleffed Nature; and Natively, our Subjection is due to Him for not only our Being, but our Well-being. Upon the other hand, the King's Power (the Government it felf, in general, being of GOD, yet the Application of it to this or that Perfon, to this or that Modell of Government, either by Election or Succeffion) is of Man, according to that, *Be fubject to every Ordinance of Man for the Lord's fake*: I fay, the cafe ftanding thus, not only in purfuance of our Allegiance to our Great and Abfolute Sovereign, are we obliged to refift what is offered and carryed on to His Difhonour; and this, leaft we fhould partake of other Men's Sins, but alfo, the People who have conferred that power, being Violented in all things that are precious to them; and the Government appointed of GOD, degenerating into Tyranny, may Recall the power given, and not only refift, but turn out fuch a Tyrant, for whofe Tyranny he had no commiffion, from them. I hope, none who will grant the Sixth Command, *Thou fhalt not Kill*, to be Binding, will refufe this. The Reafon is here, he is beyond all doubt as guilty of Murder who impowers to do the fame, as he who actually does it. Now I hope the cafe ftanding thus, all Impartial Readers will fee, how unjuftly we are condemned for owning the Lawfulnefs of Defenfive Arms; which I fhall endeavour to make yet more clear in my Application of thefe Scriptures above

bove cited, and my Anſwer to what I heard from our Antagoniſts on this Head:
And firſt, As to the People's reſiſting of *Saul*, it being an Act of Loyalty to their
Supream Sovereign, in hindering his Depute to perform a Raſh and Sinful Oath.
I wonder with what confidence, that Man, (if he be one) or rather Monſtrous
Jeſuitical Atheiſt, Biſhop *Paterſon*, could ſay to my Glorified Brother, *John
Wilſon*, (whoſe Murder is yet recent) That he doubted if they did right in ſo
doing. Sure I am, the Juſtice Clerk will not ſay ſo, who has granted that the
Almighty GOD is Supream ; and conſequently, that Subjects dare not without
Sin, ſuffer any thing to be done to His diſhonour, that is in their Power to hin-
der ; and that to Swear a Raſh Oath, obliging to Murder, is of this Nature, I
hope I ſhall not need to prove. And Secondly, As to that of *Rehoboam*, that
Tyrannical Wretch, ſhaking off all Fear of GOD, and rejecting the *Council of the
Old Men*, to his own Ruine ; that the Subjects were in their Duty in caſting him
off, I hope none will refuſe, who knows what Intereſt the People have in making
of Kings ; and that none needs to be ignorant of, who will be pleaſed to read the
17 Chapter of *Deuteronomy*, from the 14th Verſe to the End : As alſo, that the
People are bound in their Stations to oppoſe the Tyranny of their Princes, leaſt
they may ſhare with them in their Judgments. Tyranny and Oppreſſion being
a palpable Violation of the Laws of Our Bleſſed and Supream Lawgiver. Thirdly,
As to that of *Uzziah*, that he becoming ſtrong and lifted up, in meddling beyond
his Sphere with the matters of GOD, is given for the Ground of the Reſiſtance
he met with : And ſure in our caſe, our King has yet been more ſtrong and
more lifted up (I fear to his Deſtruction) in ſo far as the former did only offer
to perform ſome Office that was only peculiar to the Prieſts, but never offered to
overturn the Worſhip of GOD, of his own Appointment; and to introduce an
other diametrically oppoſite to the Revealed Will of GOD, as it is in our caſe.

Now I ſay, our King having out done *Uzziah* in his affronted Rebellion againſt
Heaven, who can blame the People if in ſtanding to their own defence they
Endeavour to aſſert that our Beſſed God is abſolute Soveraign and Maſter, and
that nothing Commanded nor impoſed, expreſly contrary to his will, which we
ſtill hold to be our Supream Law, can be binding upon them, this will be yet
more clear as what we Aſſerted a little above, that Kings and Subjects are but
Subjects to the Supream Majeſty, if you conſider that after he is thruſt out of
the Temple, he is put in a ſeveral Houſe upon the account of his Leproſie, that
which was likewiſe done to the meaneſt Subject he had in the like caſe, and what
if the Miniſtery in the Church of *Britain* and *Ireland*, imitating this Laudable
example, when ever they perceived that Dreadfull Plague of a more dangerous
Nature then Leproſie, and yet more Infectious (which I take to have been the
reaſon of their Separation) I mean our Kings horrible Adulteries, Perjuries,
publick and Private Oppoſitions to the Almighty, with that Abominable endeavour to introduce *Popery* (anent which you may ſee more in my now Glorified
Brother *John Wilſon* his Teſtimony) I ſay what if they had by a Sentance of
Excommunication ſet him apart by himſelf? And what if the People had owned
them by ſo doing ? Sure I know none that has the leaſt ſmack of Religion would
have Condemned this, and I pray God the Miniſtery yet living, may be brought
to the Senſe of their guilt in omitting this, but whatever be in this, ſure I am
the

the people Violented for not Concurring in thefe Abominations, cannot be Condemned for ftanding to their own Defence. This will be yet further clear to any who confiders what I have offered by the Enemies of our Bleffed Lord for my Satisfaction in this matter. And firft, Having made ufe of our Bleffed Lords Precept to his Difciples, when about to leave them in a Perfecuting World to wit. But now, he that has no Sword let him Sell his Coat and Buy one. Sir *William Paterfon* told me the fame, that he told my abovementioned Brother, to wit that there was meant the Sword of the Spirit, to which I Anfwered, were thefe two Swords of the Spirit Produced by the Difciples, faying here are two, were thefe two Swords of the Spirit? To this he replys no more then the Stone of the Wall behind him; And now further, I would advife that Gentleman as he tenders his Souls Eternall Well-being, that he feek Repentance of God for this fo horridly Blafphemous Expreffion, which is no other, then to Charge our Bleffed Lord with Commanding of *Simon*, how Hainous a Sin this is, I leave to any tender Confcience to confider.

Next, that Gentleman Mr. *Banerman* who they faid Reprefented the Kings Advocat there, of whom e're I proceed further I muft tell you my thoughts, I thought indeed he there Reprefented the Devil, I think not Groundlefly for the Devil you know is ftiled the Accufer of the Bretheren, how near he Refembled him I leave to the Readers confideration; Another thing faid of the Devils is they Believe and Tremble, whether this Gentleman Believes or not, I fhall not Determine, but fure I am he he Trembled and fo Repeating my Conceffions offers this Defence a good felf Defence that he has heard of felf Defence betwixt fingle Men, but there was no felf Defence by Multitudes againft Law; I think indeed to Repeat this vain Defence Refutation Sufficient, but confuting the Advantage of others I fhall divide it, it is in it felf in two parts, the firft is this Man feems to yeeld that one Man may Legally Defend himfelf againft another, and what if he be not able to prove that two or three of us were ftill againft one? I hope if he prove not this againft all, he muft Liberate all that were not Chargeable with this, and fo was bound to have Defended me conform to his own conceffion, I think this Gentleman fhould have Condecended who thefe priviledged Perfons are that they may Defend themfelves and who not; But to the Second Branch that there is no felf Defence by Multitudes againft Law Juftifiable, where was this Mans Memory that he will have my Innocent and juft felf Defence againft Law? Did I not tell him Immediately before that there could be no Law againft exprefs Texts of Scripture? And that I might the better prove this Defired they would grant to me, that the Word of God was the Supream Law to which all other Laws behoved to ftrike and vail; now this being Refufed me and nothing in the leaft offered for my Satisfaction, I hope none will Doubt but thefe Men Avowedly before the Face of the Sun fet themfelves and their Laws up above our God and his Laws, fo that all I have for the Ground of my Sentence upon the Matter is this, though God himfelf hath faid you are Right and though his Word which you call his Law fay fo too, yet we have a Law and by this Law you moft Dye, who would not Rejoice in a fentence of this Nature, that does fo nearly Refemble that Blafphemous one paffed upon his Bleffed felf? *Biefs O my Soul the Lord thy God*, there is an Expreffion in my Subfcribed Declaration,

which

which I know our Enemies upon Chrifts Account do not a litle ftartle at and I am Apprehenfive may, feem harfh to fome of our reall Friends upon miftake, the Expreffion is this, that the Enemies invafion made at *Pentland* and *Bothwel* for the Adhering to their duty was Service done to the Devil, and the Lords Peoples Innocent felf Defence being fo Affautled, was Service done to God. For Satisfaction both of Friends and Foes in this matter I fhall offer to your Confideration what follows.

I hope our Enemies themfelves will not deny, the *Presbyterian* Minifters of the Church of *Britain* and *Ireland*, to be Faithful Minifters of Chrift Jefus, if they do, they fhould have done us the Juftice to have intimate the fame with the Grounds thereof: Sure I am the behaviour of the groffeft of them would feem to cry aloud the contrary, when they come to a Death Bed where rejecting thefe perjured, Atheiftical, blafphemous. Hirelings, they call for a *Presbyterian* Minifter, witnefs, Mr. *John Elis* and the laft Chancellor with many others, I hope none of our Friends doubt this, fo then we fhall take this for granted.

Well then (if they be Minifters as we moft firmly hold) efpecially having nothing from our Enemies to the the contrary, but rather a firm Confirmation as, I have faid, I hope ye will grant me alfo, that they are bound to obey that Commiffion in the laft of *Matth.* two laft *Verfes*, *Go ye therefore and teach all Nations, baptizing them in the Name of the Father, and of the Son, and of the Holy Ghoft, teaching them to obferve all things whatfoever I have commanded you, and lo, I am with you always unto the end of the World Amen.* I hope I need ufe no Argument to reinforce this, this being the Command and Commiffion of our bleffed Lord Jefus Chrift in it felf fufficient to bind all, and needing the fuffer-age of no Mortal; Let it ftand as a fure Truth then, that our Minifters are Chrift's Servants, and that our bleffed Lords Commiffion to them to Preach is ftill binding, and fhall be to the Worlds end. I hope I fhall need to be at little pains to prove, that by that fame Commiffion the Lords People are obliged to hear; I hope none will doubt this whoever has Read that Word, *Rom.* 10. 14. *How can they hear without a Preacher.* Now the cafe being thus, that our Minifters are Minifters, and by vertue af their Commiffion they are bound to Preach, and confequently we bound to hear, and that under no lefs Hazard then refufing Obedience to one of the laft Precepts of our bleffed Lord and Mafter Jefus Chrift. I hope none who owns my firft Principle will yet fay, that any Mortal can invalidate this Commiffion, or hinder the due performance of this fo abfolutely neceffary and indifpenfible a Duty, to which we are the more Encouraged to yeild Voluntare Obedience becaufe of his Promifed Prefence therein to the end of World, I fay none will fay fo, that Beleives there is a God, if any fay that this Satisfies not as to the gathering together in Multitudes and going to the Fields I hope this will have litttle Weight with any that Confiders this was practice of our Bleffed Mafter and his Apoftles they being Acted by an Infallible Spirit, and fo their Example is a Sufficient Warrand, and our Bleffed Lord himfelf being God-man, and fo Effentially elevated above all Sufpition of being Miftaken, I fay thefe Sufficiently Warrand this. If it be further Objected, but why are you there in Arms? I Anfwer firft, We have our Bleffed Mafters Precept for it in the 22 of *Luke* the 36 Verfe, in thefe Words, *But now he that hath a Purfe let him take it, and likewife his Scrip, and he that hath no Sword let*

hin

him Sell his Garment and Buy one; Now having removed what has been offered by our Enemies againſt this, we ſhall ſtudy in the Lords Strength to reinforce our Argument therefrom: And firſt I would have you notice the Emphaſis in the words, but now as if he had ſaid my time in the World here is to be as to us a peaceable time, what I am to ſuffer here being Tranſacted betwixt me and my Father before the Foundation of the World, and I being obliged in the Room of loſt Mankind, to take on me Fleſh and Blood, and all Human Frailties, ſin only Excepted, that I may be a Compleat Saviour, this being my free offering to my Father ; and conſequently I being to perform all · that is requiſite herein, not only freely but cheerfully, therefore during this time there is no hurry to be made in the World upon my account, and I atteſt your ſelves if in following of me, even conform to this method you have found your ſelves at any Diſadvantage in wanting either Purſe, Scrip or Sword : But now, now that I am going to leave you after that I have Performed, that which was tranſacted betwixt the Father and me before the World was founded; you are not to be ſo paſſive would he ſay as before, that being contained in the Belly of the Fathers Tranſaction and mine, and therefore I command him that wants a Sword to Sell his Garment and Buy one. Now as to this Sword, our Bleſſed Lord commands his Diſciples to Buy, and in them all that ſhall Succeed them to the end of the World (for I ſuppoſe our Enemies will not ſay this Command was given them as Miniſters, leaſt thereby they ſhould wrong *Cæſar*) being commanded them as Chriſtians, I demand our Enemies, what theſe Diſciples were to do with their Swords, for my part I know nothing, if it were not either to offend or Defend or both I expect they will not readily ſay, either to offend or both (though I humbly conceive they ſhould not err much in ſo ſaying, eſpecially if they conſider aright the Penult *Pſalm*, then they muſt ſay to me, that it was to defend, and if to defend be in any caſe lawfull as I am ſure it is, then in our caſe, I am confident none will refuſe it, who has read and conſidered what I have ſaid before.

Secondly, we have · the Example of *Abraham* for this in the 14 of the *Geneſis*, where in a caſe nothing ſo favourable as ours he practiſes Self-Defence, and I hope the moſt daring of our Adverſaries ſhall not dare to condemn him for it.

Thirdly that Scripture, *When you are Perſecuted in one City flee to another,* Helps in this caſe to ſatisfie what we have ſaid, and in this I have the ſuffrage of the *Engliſh* Law made uſe of by Sir *George M·kenzie* in his Criminals, whereby the Defendant is declared innocent if to evidence his Defence, he have fled ſome few Steps, and who doubts but when flight will not do, the Defendant may reſiſt by Force : To all this if you add the practice of all Reformed Churches, and the preſent practice of the *Hungarians,* I hope I ſhall find, you have not had the beſt Ground to queſtion our going to the Fields to hear the Word of GOD preached in Arms, eſpecially conſidering that this was a practice we were forced to from abſolute neceſſity, ſeing that our being in Houſes rendered us more lyable to be a prey to our Enemies, Now I hope whoever ſeriouſly ponders what the Lord has given for Defence, here will not think that we were ſerving God in theſe Meetings, which I with all confidence averr we were, and bleſs the Lord that not only I, but not a few thouſands in *Scotland* has it to ſay to the Commendation of his free Grace, and commendation of this ſo much commended

mended way, that we have found our Lord as good as his Word, in being with and Countenancing us; and this being so, I doubt as little to averr, that the Assaulters upon this account, coming in a Hostile manner, without the least provocation upon our part, were in that serving the Devil, for who but the Devil would give Orders to fire upon a People in the actual Worship of GOD, for no other reason, but because they were so doing.

Among the other things, that through the brittleness of my Memory I have omitted, this which I have got from another hand, is one; That after Sentence, I Attested the Lord, that ever since I understood what Treason and Rebellion were, I had ever abhorred both Treason and Traitors, Rebellion and Rebells : To which their Answer was, that every word I spake was Treason ! To this I Replyed, that I was sorry that what my blessed Lord and Master accepted off my hand as indispensible Duty, should be by his Deputies and Servants reputed Rebellion.

I must add here also, that in my Conference with Sir *William Paterson*, against my Assertion of Christ's Headship of the Church, he offered this Answer, that he knew that Christ was Head of the Invisible Church, insinuating, that the King or any other they pleased might be Head to the Visible.

To this my Answer is, I fear this Gentleman has wronged himself more than he is aware of, for having renounced Christ Jesus my blessed Lord and Master, to be Head of that Church, of which he owns himself a Member, he does more than faintly insinuate, there are no Members of the Invisible Church amongst them, for if they were, they would hold Christ to be their Head, and in so doing, do nothing but what is their Duty. But I would ask this Gentleman, whether he looks upon our blessed Lord's Commission to his Disciples, as a sufficient Warrand for them to manage all the Affairs of the Visible Church ? and where he has his Warrand from the Magistrates medling further in Church Affairs, than to see what is ordered by the God of Heaven, exactly done to the Glory of the God of Heaven; which I look upon as a Power *Circa sacra*, and not *in sacris*. Sure I am, all that have any thing of the Exercise of their Reason, will say he was bound to me in these. But whatever his Sentiments be in these Matters, I am confident that our blessed Lord and Master in this Commission to his Ministers to Preach and Baptize, gave them Commission also to exercise Discipline and Government, since the one cannot consist without the other; and that as to the Obedience to this Commission, they are lyable to Answer to none even in their visible Estate; But our blessed Lord Jesus Christ, their and our blessed Lord and Master and Head, anent which the Magistrates Power is only Cumulative not Privative. For further clearing of this, I hope Sir *William Paterson* will not refuse it, that our blessed Lord was Head of that Church whereof *Judas* was a Member, and if so his fancy of Christ's being only the Head of the Invisible Church will be found a meer Chimera ; For I doubt nothing to averr, that under our blessed Lord and Master in his Visible Church there is no other Power granted to any Mortals but to his Ministers of his own Appointment, whom he has cloathed with a Ministerial Power conjunctly under him, to act in his Affairs as they shall answer to him their only Head: and though amongst these his Ministers, thus by him impowered, there may and

ought

ought to be a Superiority of Order for Decency, yet amongſt them we find no
Warrand in all the Word of God for a Superiority of Juriſdiction, as is practiſed among that *Prelatical* Party, who have to this Abomination; added that
other of the Renouncing of Chriſt to be their Head, and with the ſame Breath, to
the aſtoniſhment of all that have the leaſt impreſſion of a Deity, have ſworn
the contrary in their *Teſt*.

Now my Lords of Juſticiary, and you the Aſſizers here Sworn, I hope no Man
who hath any thing left of the Exerciſe of his reaſon will deny, that you were
bound in Conſcience (if you know there is any ſuch thing) and in all Law, E-
quity and reaſon to have given me Satisfaction, not only as to what I have hinted
at by way of Defence for my ſelf, but alſo to have ſatisfied me with a Satisfactory
Anſwer to what is ſtanding on record, left by our Country Man Mr. *Rutherfoord*,
a very Eminent Light in his time, and one much Countenanced of the Lord in
his Books called *Lex Rex*, due Right of Presbytery, and his Peaceable Plea;
as alſo in that Book Entitled *Jus divinum miniſterij Evangelici*, Writen by our
Faithfull and very Reverend, and Dearly Beloved Brethren the Miniſters of *Lon-
don*, and as Eminently worthy and Reverend Mr. *George Gilleſpie* his Aſſertion
of Church Government, with his *Aarons* Rod; as alſo in the Apologie, writen
by the two Reverend and Worthy Divines Mr. *Hugh Smith* and Mr. *Alexander
Jamiſon*, and in the Apologetical Relation, *Naphtali*, *Jus Populi*, and ſeveral
others, in all which you will find theſe Principles and Practices, I have Aſſerted owned, and offered my ſelf in the ſtrength of my Bleſſed Lord to Defend,
whether in my Principle or Additionall Declarations and Teſtimonies, fully,
Solidly and Satisfactorily, to all Unbyaſſed and unprejudicate Perſons aſſerted,
Proven, Vindicated and clearly made out from the word of God (which I yet
aſſert to be the Supream Law) the Law of Nature, and the Law of Nations;
found reaſon, and ſolid Senſe: and ſince it is ſo, which all the World muſt grant,
and you eſpecially who refuſe me Satisfaction hereanent, by your either Total
ſilence, or if ſpeaking any thing at all, againſt theſe things what you have ſaid, is
either Blaſphemy or Nonſenſe. I ſay the whole Unbyaſſed World would acknowledge and firmly aſſent, you were bound to give ſatisfaction as to theſe
things; eſpecially conſidering, any Anſwer has been given to any of theſe, has
been the burning of ſome of theſe Books by the hands of a Hangman in a Fire,
a very ſorry Anſwer indeed ; but however, of a peice with the reſt of your fightings againſt the Almighty : And how durſt you, for your Souls, offer to Fire ſuch
Books, ſo ſolidly digeſted by ſuch precciouſly Worthy and Eminent Authors ?
If it had not been to ſhew your deſpite to the Spirit of GOD, and ſhew that you
will ſtill go on in Rebellion againſt Heaven, and who knows not that the burn-
ers of Books founded on the Word of GOD, have more than enough of Incli-
nation to burn that Holy and Bleſſed Word it ſelf? And indeed I think it not
ſtrange to ſee Men poſting hard to *Rome*, as you are doing, to vent your Inclina-
tions that way, ſince it is not a few Years ſince many of your ſharpeſt Friars,
found you to be Men of the ſame Kidney with the *Anti-Chriſt* himſelf, that
Whore who ſits upon the Head of many Waters, whoſe Judgment lingers not.
And if any beſide a Fire, has been offered againſt any of theſe, it has been by o-
thers ſo cleanly wiped off, that theſe Books ſtands ſtill in Vigour, and ſo do all

my

my Affertions and Principles for any thing I have seen or heard to the contrary. Now I leave it to all the impartial in the World, to judge what Affront is here offered to the Almighty, in cutting off one of his Creatures? To our King, in cutting off one of his Subjects? Who to this Hour, never heard a Challenge for Difloyalty, if it were not from such as makes Loyalty Difloyalty, & Sin Duty; which Challenge I very chearfully bear, being fufficiently perfwaded of the unjuftnefs thereof, and to Nature in cutting off of their fellow Creatures: and all this without so much as a Hearing of what he had to fay for himfelf; or any thing of an Anfwer to any of thofe who has fufficiently Vindicated all thefe Principles and Practices, for which he was upon the Pannal; and yet in this matter are thefe poor Men more guilty in this refpect, that they refufe the Pannal the benefite of fuch Defences, as he had very good ground to believe fhould have been offered by the Almighty himfelf, conform to his Promife of giving in that Hour whatfoever fhould be neceffary for any of his, in my Cafe, (I mean ftanding before Rulers and great Men to bear Teftimony to the Truth) I fay, I being helped of my Blefled LORD to Act Faith on His Promife, and finding my Blefled LORD and Mafter prefent by his Spirit to have performed the fame, and I having intimated fo much to them (as you may fee above) How durft thefe difpifers of GOD refufe me the benefite of thefe Defences (if this be not to declare open Hoftility againft Heaven, I know not what is) and fince it is fo, as I can with confidence affert it was, and the very enemies themfelves (if they had not been dangeroufly hardened) could not but have felt it to be, for which my Soul fhall ever blefs his Name; and I hope I fhall not be left alone here, expecting the affiftance of not a few in thefe Nations in this matter, who have in this particular, to the refrefhment of their Souls, found a new Proof of our GOD's being the Hearer of Prayer. I fay again, thefe things being fo, I hope none who are not engaged in the fame rage againft GOD, with thefe his Enemies and ours, upon his Account will doubt but their whole procedure againft me in this matter has been a Decreed and intended Murder, not only againft me, but alfo my Blefled LORD and Mafter in and through me. And leaft any fhould miftake me here, let them but confider thefe Three Scriptures. Firft, *He that touches you, touches the Aple of mine Eye.* Secondly, *In all their Afflictions he was Afflicted.* Thirdly, *Paul, Paul, Why perfecuteft thou me?* And I hope the miftake fhall be rubbed off. And now having through the Blefling and Affiftance of the Almighty, gotten my Teftimony brought to this Pafs, that the cafe betwixt his People and them is clearly ftated; to evidence, that not only I, but fuch others of our perfwafion, all the Nations over; are indeed Chriftians, I refolve in the LORD'S ftrength, as he fhall affift, to leave behind me a Teftimony of my Tendernefs, both to the Souls and Bodies, of fuch as has given no fmall Proof of their Thirfting after my blood, in dealing with them, as follows:

And now, unto his Majefty our King, muft I Addrefs my felf, and to all under him, from his Brother the Duke of *York*, to all the Counfellors, whether Publick or Secret, in the Three Kingdoms; and under them, to all the Sheriffs, Juftices, with their Clerks and Pendicles of Court, even to thefe of the meaneft Office (I mean the Dempfters) and after thefe, to the whole Magiftrates of Burrows with their Pendicles to the loweft; and then to all the Members of thefe

Part

Parliaments, fince his Majefty's Reftauration, whether fuch as did fit there by Birth, or were Elected; and as to thefe Elected, even to their Electors: and in a Word, to all and fundry who have concurred with, Homologate or Ratified your Uniuft Sentences pronunced againft the Almighty, whether more directly, or at leaft in his Members.

Now, as to you all and fundry, I declare in the Entry of my Addrefs, as in the fight of *Jehovah*, whofe I am, and before whom both you and I, e're long, muft ftand naked and bare, to anfwer for all we have done in the Flefh, That my defign in this my Addrefs, next to the Glory of GOD, the Good and Edification of his People, and confequently the advancement of his Work. The Third thing which the LORD my GOD has held before my Eves in all this my Trial, has been your Conviction from the higheft to the loweft, if poffible; and that I may the better reach that end my Bleffed LORD has determined my Heart to follow this Method, *Firft*, To deal more particularly with you in laying before your eyes the Egregioufnefs of your Sin. *Secondly*, To Expoftulate with you to return from the fame to GOD'S Glory, and your own Souls Eternal well-being. And *Thirdly*, And if in this I prevail not, to remonftrate the hazard of refufing this my Warning. And *Fourthly*, To take Inftruments upon what the LORD by me, the Unworthieft of his Servants, has been doing for you, and of your Refufal (I mean as to fo many as fhall be fo far left of the LORD, as to refufe the fame, and Oh! that there might be few fuch) then I am to leave my Companions in Tribulation, and Brethren in our ever Bleffed and Eldeft Brother Chrift Jefus, the LORD of Glory with a word of Exhortation, and fo Conclude,

Now, Great Sir, for to you and all under you, and who inftigate you to, and concurred with you in thefe Soul-deftroying Practices, I am in the ftrength of *Jehovah* to remonftrate, I Addrefs my felf, and in the firft place, muft take the liberty to tell you in the Name of my great Lord and Mafter Jefus Chrift, that it is not unknown to your Majefty, nor any of thefe to whom I Addrefs my felf, jointly with you, that not only at your Coronation, your Majefty and all under you, from the higheft to the loweft, but alfo before thefe whole Nations were, and yet are engaged in a moft Solemn Covenant with the Ever-Living GOD, Party Contracter on the one hand, and your Majefty and all under you in thefe Nations, from the higheft to the loweft; on the other hand, to the obfervance of which Covenant, thefe Nations and all in them, fhall forever be bound and obliged, from the higheft to the loweft, while Sun and Moon endures; neither is there any imaginable way of Diffolving the fame, efpecially confidering, that therein our Obligation being only to Amend our Lives, and to Worfhip the Almighty GOD, conform to his own Appointment, and to oppofe our felves, our Lives and Fortunes, to all courfes and ways inconfiftent with thefe ends; thefe being Moral Duties to which we were Antecedently bound, as is the Nature alfo of all thefe Duties we are obliged to by thefe Covenants. Now Great Sir, the Cafe being thus, I hope ye will not judge your felf obliged to fuch as makes this Defence for breaking of thefe Covenants, that your Majefty was forced thereto, for indeed I look upon it as a great imputation upon your Majefty efpecially being Stiled *Defender of the Faith*, to have been in any meafure under either Neceffity or Conftraint, to have joined in a Duty fo abfolutly neceffary,

and

and if there was any thing of force where was the Intimation thereof? fure
I am there was nothing thereof publickly to be feen, and yet giving but not
granting it had been fo your Majefty and all under you; were unexpreffibly
more obliged to the performance therefore, then were the People of Ifreal to
the performance of that made with the Gibeonites as may be feen above, nor
fhall I think your Majefty will think your felf obliged to them, who fhould
for Vindication of your Breach of thefe Covenants offer this Defence, that
your Majefty is under Covenant of a pofterior date bound to the Pope and fome
of his Creatures to introduce Popery, and to Emancipate thefe Territories to
that Antichriftian Yoke, if any fuch thing be, as, the Carriage of the Court
this confiderable time too loudly infinuates, Sure I am it were more for your
Majefties Honour, and the Glory of God, and the good of your Nations to
break that Covenant than to keep it, it being a Covenant made againft the Almighty, which by no imaginable pretence can be juftified; but leaving thefe
things to your Majefties confideration, and to the confideration of fuch as may
with you be concerned herein: I muft make bold to ask again, by what Authority you came to Diffolve this Contract? (yea I may fay and that upon
good Grounds as Glorious a Contract as ever was made on Earth, while Adhered to of as Glorious effects) I fay I muft make bold to ask by what Authority this is broken? and unlefs you be fo bold as to run your felf upon
Boffes of the Buckler of the Almighty, in refufing that which the Juftice
Clerk but faintly granted (which the Lord avert) I mean unlefs you deny
Jehovah to be Supreme Lord and Mafter of Heaven and Earth; and all the
Kings and Governors in the Earth to be his Deputies and Servants, I fhall
defy you or any Mortal to fatisfy me in this, if you confider what is faid before on this Subject, and what is contained in the feveral Authors abovementioned on this Matter, Now we fhall take it for granted, that thefe Covenants
ftands ftill binding, and I am fure we have good ground fo to do, for any
thing we have either read or heard to the contrary. Then great Sir muft
I in the next place ask, how it comes to pafs, that over the belly of thefe Covenants Fpifcopacy and Eraftianifme (againft which as to the unlawfulnefs
thereof, and their inconfiftency with the Word of God, who have fo many
Teftimonies ftanding in Record, not only in the Word of God, but in other
Humane Writings, drawn and founded thereupon, without the leaft fatisfacti-
on offered by our Adverfaries) come to be introduced amongft us who be-
fide the unlawfulnefs of the things themfelves have this to fay, that we have
Sworn with Hands lifted up to the Almighty, not only never to join with,
but with our Lives and Fortunes to oppofe either, I fay how comes thefe
not only to be introduced, but we by Armed force Hunted, Haraffed, Plun-
dered, Tortured and Hailed to Scaffolds, for no other Reafon, but our refufing? Anent which the unlawfulnefs of the things were to us fufficient Warrand though we had not been in Covenant, but much more being under the
fame, as for my part I can Dream of no Reafon for introducing of thefe, being ftrangers in the Church of Chrift, not only in his own bleffed time, and
the time of the Apoftles who furvieved him; But alfo for three hundred
Years thereafter, Nor do I ever hear or Read that any other ufe they were

introduced but for that *Antichrist*, that Man of Sin his Exaltation, being made ufe of the one for his Advancement is that damnable absolute Supremacy of his in the Church, and the other for the fame end in the State, and truely if this be the thing, it does not a little confirm me in the Belief of that fecond Covenant you and your Brother have made with the Pope, which I mentioned a little above.

But I fay, How, come the Subjects of *Britain* and *Ireland*, to be forced to a Complyance with thefe? Sure, you fay by your Principles, that you allow not of the forcing of Mens Confciences by the Sword, looking upon it as a *Turkish* way, as Prelate *Paterfon* faid to my lately Martyred Brother, *John Wilfon*, and why are you worfe than *Turks*, in this violently Practifing, contrary to your Principles. In the next place, I come to enquire at your Majefty, why this Monftruous abominable Teft, which the *Turk* himfelf could not but Scunner at, is not only Enacted to be taken by all his Majefties Subjects here in *Scotland*, but alfo by Violence and force obtruded on many both Gentle and Semple, Rich and Poor ! Why this is done I cannot Divine, if it be not to let the World fee, you mind to out-do Proud *Pharoch*, in daring the Almighty ? And why, Pray you, is there a thing called, An Act made Difcharging People to Affociate together upon any pretence whatfoever, for their own innocent and neceffary felf Defence without your Majefties fpecial Command, and this alfo Sworn to in that horred Teft? It is not unknown to any, that there may many Emergents fall out, that may make this, which is by that pretended Law, made no lefs than Treafon, become a moft neceffar and indifpenfible Duty, as in the cafe of a fudden Invafion by an Enemy, your Majefty being at a great diftance, and who knows, but the Alarm may be keeped from your Majefty by fome keeped about Court for that end ? Who doubts, but in fuch a Cafe, abfolute Neceffity will become a Law to the People ? And who doubts, but if for fear of this Law any fhould ly by, but they might be arraigned as yet greater Traitors? And if in this cafe this fhould be juftifiable, why not in ours, being fo inhumanly Affaulted by a company of Murdering *Papifts*, *Atheifts*, or worfe ? And for any thing we know, his Majefty being all this while a great ftranger to our Affairs, through the induftry of fome difaffected to the way of GOD, who are keeped about Court for that end ; I fay this, as alfo that by the Inftigation of fuch, there is a pretended Law made, Difcharging any under the Pain of Treafon to meet or Confult, in order to the Remonftrating of our Cafe to his Majefty, will to all unbyaffed, fufficiently Warrand our innocent felf Defence, as to what may be objected againft this, having hinted a little in the fore part of my Teftimony, and the whole of our bufinefs in thefe being fufficiently juftified by the feveral Authors abovementioned without any Anfwer as yet. I fay again, Why are all thefe things done ? And now further, let me ask at your Majefty, Why are our Prifons keeped ftill throng with Prifoners, fome Aged, fome Infirm and Tender, fome out of Capacity to mantain themfelves, for no other caufe, but that they defire to keep a Confcience void of Offence towards GOD and towards Man, and fome Honourable Ladies alfo, for no other Reafon, than for Refetting and hearing of fome honeft and faithfull Minifters in their Houfes, or Refetting

or

or Refreshing some of the LORD'S People in their Necessities, I am sure none who ever read the 25 Chapter of *Matthew* from the 31st Verse to the end, will look upon this as a capital Crime, but as an indispensible Duty. I say it again, why are all these things done? is it to satisfie these Blood-thirsty Prelats of yours, or some of the Popish Party whom your Brother has flocking about him in Swarms?

Great, Sir all these small Sins? And besides are these Innumerable other Sins, have you and all these, to whom with youI Address my self to answer for, and that the Weight thereof may be a little better laid open to your Majesty, and these others I pray be at the pains with me to Recapitulate the same yet once more, it is no small Sin do you think to break the Covenant with GOD and to force your Subjects to do also? Is it no small sin to cast off the way of GOD, and to Banish that Religion of his own Appointment, and introduce that amongst us, which both your Majesty and all under you have Vomited up and thrown out by that Solemn Oath? Is it no small Sin do you think to Impose Contradictory Oaths upon your People and so to force them to open Rebellion against the Almighty? Is it no small thing to Tye your People as it were with Fetters of Iron, till they get their Throats cut by that Atheisticall, Papisticall, Malignant party, to whom you have lent your Ear, now these two and Twenty Years and refuse all hearing to your most faithful and Loving Subjects, I mean such as are desiring as to give the Almighty GOD what is due, in the next Place to give *Cesar* what is his, are all these small Faults think you? Is it a small thing think you to strive with the Son of GOD for State, and to presume to thrust him out of his Chair in his Church which is his due as only head thereof? And yet to cause your Subjects Swear this is horrid Blasphemy. Is it no small Sin think you to lift up your self above the Almighty, and to set up your Humane Laws above his Divine ones? I say are all these small Sins? If you either say or think, so I must take leave to tell you, I differ from you in Judgement, and must further tell you my Sentiments thereof, and indeed great Sir, I look upon all these things as most Horrid Acts of Rebellion againsi the Almighty, what Sir if the meanest of these Intrusted by your Majesty in any Publick trust, had offered the Thousand part of that Indignity to your Majesty, as to have openly and Avowedly before the Sun torn, a Contract betwixt your Majesty, and the rest of your Subjects; and told all your Subjects, that from this his Deed they were obliged to joyn with him, in this same Contempt of your Majesty, and should have further told your Majesty's Subjects, that your Power and Authority wsa to Cede to his, and that your Majesties just Laws made in free Parliaments, were to vail their Cape to his petty Acts, and so forth of the rest, would not your Majesty have thought such a Person stark Mad, and have caused drag him out as a Traitor and Rebell (and that justly,) for so doing.

And truely, whatever might have Justifyed your Majesty in so doing, can not but Infinitely, more justify our most Glorious GOD in Serving your Majest-, and all under you who have Concurred in this Rebellion, at that Rate of Draging you forth, and giving you your Portion with the Workers of Iniquity, this will be the more clear, if your Majesty consider what I have hinted before, and what is more fully contained in the Author abovementioned, and this your hor-

rid

rid Rebellion againſt the Almighty, is not a little Aggravat
able Reſtauvatiòn you was Tryſted with ſo immediatel
what was this your return, for that ſo ſignall Providence
think, that in this you were in your Duty ; I hope by this
is rightly Airted where to find out the Traitors and Rebe
ons, even there where ny are who have Inſtigated, and C
jeſty to this Horrid Rebellion, whoever they be, if it wer
the Duke of *York*, to the meaneſt under your Majeſty, n
Meaſure laid before your Majeſty, the Greivouſneſs of the
your Majeſty, and theſe to whom with your Majeſty, I Ac
ed to charge your ſelves, and Mourn, For I am in the nex
ſecond part of of my Task, which your Majeſty may Remen
ate with you for a return from the ſame to GOD's Glory, ;
Eternal Well-being, which in the Aſſiſtance of my GOD, l
   Now let me obteſt you all in the Bowels of my Bleſſed I
you have any Reſpect to the Glory of GOD, to the Eterna
own Immortall Souls. to the well being of your Poſterity, a
well being of theſe Nations of which you are all Members (
Sizes) in the fear of GOD that you wobld lay a ſide your Er
and followed that Advice given in the Second *Pſalm* from
Cloſe, and that you may be the better helped to this Read a
whole *Pſalm*, not forgetting to pray over your Meditations
ſome time a part for conſidering the greatneſs of the Affronts
in all theſe Acts and Actions, we have been weakly hintirg
in, your Unparalleled Deſpite done to the Spirit of God, in
ſo palpably againſt the Almighty, and ſetting up your Mo
above that unerring Law of his, I mean his Bleſſed will Re
as alſo the Weight of the Blood you have Engaged your Sho
ceuting theſe your Abominable wicked Laws, which is no
Blood-ſhed, ſince the Blood of Righteous *Abel* to this very l
er thar Paſſage in the 23 of *Mathew*, from the 29 to the
Faithfull you are or any of you ſhall be helped to be in Jud
this matter, the greater hope in your caſe, I pray God none
ſo your ſelves, as to offer to ſhift off this Charge, which I
never have gaound to do till you have Solidly Anſwered all
Word of GOD, for binding the ſame upon you, as alſo in
and amongſt the reſt in this poor and Feckleſs eſſay of mi
as in the ſight of GOD I have Ventured upon, next to the
the good of his people, with an Eye to the Everlaſting Well
one and all of you, even of my moſt inveterate Enemy, M
of *Edinburgh* as you call him, and becauſe neither time wi
ſo properly my Task, l Recommend it to you for your help
Writings of our Faithful Divines, both in *Britain* and *Irelan*
meet with what may before your better help in this ind
duty, and whither I come ſpeed or not I muſt adviſe you al
this matter ſuch of your faithfull Miniſters as are yet amon

you fhould Eſſay this in the time of your Health, which not a few of you have ventured upon at your Death fearing that then it may prove too late, for feldom is late Repentance fure Repentance : Now if you fhall be helped of the Lord to grant me this my Suit which is fo much for the Glory of GOD, the good of your own Soul, the good of your Pofterity and of the Lands wherein you live, I do nothing doubt but e're all be done you fhall find Rea- fon to blefs the Lord, and to alter your Sentiments not only of me, but of all who with me have been fo tender of your Souls as not to dare to harden you in your finful Courfes by Concurring and going alongft with you in thefe fo Horrid Abominations, and fhall not only think but find it verifyed upon your Spirits, that we have been (that which we are indeed) the only Faith- ful and Loyal Subjects in thefe Dominions, endeavouring in our Stations to render to the Almighty GOD what is his, and to *Cæfar* what is his, which is true Loyalty indeed ; For we dare not Join with thefe that have in their rage againft GOD combined with his Deputes againft him, and if you fhall be yet fo far hardened as to refufe this my fo Ufeful and to you profitable Advice, Then muft I come in the third place to Remonfterate the Hazard of your Re- fufal, which cannot fail but to be upon this Account the greater that you fhall refufe a Meſſage as it were fent from the Dead unto you, and fo a greater ftep of God's Infinite Condefcendancy unto you.

Well then that in this Matter I may be the more particular with you, I fhall Obteft one and all of you to Confider what ye will do in the day of Vifitation, I mean in the great and terrible Day of the LORD (for as to particular Vifi- tations in time, it may be you have laid your Count by them, and therein done foolifhly enough to) when our bleffed Lord Jefus Chrift (againft whom ye have been raging thefe two and twenty Years, and it may be fome of you longer)fhall fet his Throne in the Clouds, and caufe found the laft Trumpet at the hearing whereof, all that ever had a being muft Anfwer and Compear, and Stand Naked before our Great King and Head of his own Church, to whom the Father has Committed the Judgment, and anfwer for what they have done in the Flefh : Which His coming is as it fhall be the the Joyfuleft fight that ever the People of the Lord did fee, fo to all the wicked it fhall be the moft dreadful and terrible day that ever their Eyes beheld, and this the rather that they could never be induced to believe the fame in time, fo it fhall be a Dreadful furprifal to them.

And now to begin with your Majefty, great Sir are you at a Point what to do in that day ? It is Poffible for what Straits you have Forecaften in time you are at a Point, to Shelter under the Wings of that Antichrift, that Man of Sin, the Pope, with fome of his Affociats as the Kings of *France* and *Spain*, and fuch others as with you have Combined againft the Lord, but what if even as to that you be Difappointed ? And what if all thefe have their hands Filled at Home, fo as they fhall not have a Man to Spare to you, to fend either to *England, Scot- land* or *Ireland*, Sure I am what ever Confidence you may have in them as to that (which the Lord himfelf Break) yet in that Day none of thefe fhall Avail you.

And for the Duke of *York*, have you Sir thought upon a Lurking Hole againft

D that

that Day ? Think not Sir to Wrap your felf in the Bloody Cloaths of thefe lately Murdered Martyrs, Noblemen and others, who by your Inftigation are Murdered, for no other Caufe, but that they have been Endeavouring the Security of the Proteftant Religion (a Duty Indifpenfibly called for at their hands) thefe fhall be fo far from being a Shelter for you, that you fhall thereby be (yet more) laid open to the juft Judgement of the Almighty.

Then for our *Scots* Cardinal, the Marquis of *Huntly*, and his Depute the Chancelor, whofe true Epithete ye may Read in the 9th. of *Jeremiah* the Latter part of the 8th. Verfe, what Dreams thir Men of hiding themfelves ? Sure they cannot be fo Infatuate as to think their Works of Supererogation (if the Murdering and Confenting to the Murder of the Lords People be fuch) fhall prove a Covering Broad enough for them.

And for that Blood Thirfty Wretch *Claver-Houfe*, how thinks he to Shelter himfelf that Day ? Is it Poffible the Pitiful thing can be fo Mad as to think to Secure himfelf by the Fleetnefs of his Horfe (a Creature he has fo much Refpect for, that he Regarded more the lofs of his Horfe at *Drumclog*, than all the Men that fell there, and Sure on either party there fell Prettier Men than himfelf) no Sure, though he could fall upon a *Chymift* that could Extract the Spirits out of all the Horfe in the World, and Infule them in his one, though he were on that Horfe Back never fo well Mounted, he need not Dream of Efcaping. Then for *Meldrum*, I think the Bignefs of his Belly will fecure him as to Trufting him in his Heels, what can he truft in ? Poffibly he has laid up in Store fo much of his Evil-Conqueft Goods, that he has Squized out of the People in *Tiviotdale*, the *Mers*, and other Places of the Nation, as he intends to Bribe Juftice that Day (a Trick too Common now a Dayes) but if this Fancy be in the head of that Belly-god, I would Undeceive him in time, for I can Affure him he will meet with a Difappointment.

Now where thinks Major *White* to Shelter, he can not Poffibly Dream of Creeping into Munfmegg, I am told fhe is Riven by fome of the Duke of *Yorks* Creatures, its like he may be feen through that Breach, but this will be found to him an Unfure hiding Place, the heat, the Vehement Heat of the Elements, that will be Melted that Day, may fo Sore affect this Shelter as he fhall be Melted out alfo.

Now for your *Scots Pallas* (I mean Sir *James Turner* another Major, a godly Leach indeed) what Dreams he to do that day, efpecially when with his former and Latter Rage againft the Almighty, he confiders that Paffage in his *Pallas armata*, wherein he does no lefs than *Spitt Venom* in the Face of our Bleffed Lord in his poor Members, telling them that fome of them will fay, Curfe ye *Meroz*, who neither know whether *Meroz* be a Man, a Town, or a Country ; Thefe are his words as I Remembered, and what if fome of the meaner fort of your Brethren, wanting the Benefite of Education, fhould have been found in this particular Ignorant ? was there any *Herefy* here ? Was it not enough for them to know, that whatever *Meroz* was, there was there a Threatening intended againft all who fhould refufe Gods Call, to help our LORD againft the Mighty and yet a far forer Wo againft all fuch as with him have Confpired to help and harden the Mighty againft the LORD, and if fome fuch fhould have been Ignorant

ant if he have been *Jackson* on the Fifth of the *Judges*, 23 *Verse*, he dare not say
all were so, I say what does this Viperous *Pallas* of ours intend that day ? can the
Body be so Mad as to think of Sheltering amongst these *Pikes* of his ? (a Weap-
on he so much Idolizes) which he must have so closely Served together, and
when all is done, he must have a Rank of Horse drawen up before them Armed all
over. Now what if this should not serve his turn even against Men? For who knows
not, that as good a Fellow as himself, being opposite to him, might command off
a Serjeant or Lieutenant, which a Commanded party of *Halbardiers*, and pos-
fibly a few *Sythes* Discharging them to return, till they have killed some of these
Horse? Sure I am in this case (which is nothing impossible) our Served *Pikes*
behoved to stand still, and so leave the Wings of Shot to advance alone (which
I think he would not do of choice) or otherwise he must come over these Horses
Tumbling before him, and so indanger his falling in that Embarrass, he is at so
much pains to Guard his Disciples against, and if this Shift of his can not secure
him against Men (and I am sure there are many Thousands in the Nation Sharp-
er sighted in these Affairs, then either he or I) how does the Mad Creature
Dream he should here secure himself against the Almighty.

And now having Touched these few particularly, because such as I have Observ-
ed to be more *Mad in Rage against the LORD, and against his Anointed than many
of their Brethren*; I insist to pose the rest anent this same Question, and in a more
General manner, anent which e're I proceed, I shall give them this Advice, not
to look upon their Sin as Specifically Different from the other, but only in de-
grees, and it may be some, I have not Named, be as far Benn in their Rage
against their Maker, as these I have Named: I am under a Necessity here to
mention that Wretched Creature (our Country-Man) the very Bane of
the Country, who if he be not as far advanced as any against our Lord, he
is not to be blamed for it; since it is not want of Good-Will, but Pith, that
keeps him back, his Name is Sir *John Whitefoord* of *Milton*, as to you with
whom I am to deal more generally, if ye be Conscious to your selves of less
Activity in this Rebellion, nor your Brethren, your work of Repentance will
be the more easie which I beg our good God may both facilitate and hasten.

I come then first to the Members of Parliament, that have been under our
King the great Agents in all this lamentable Catastrophe, whether such as are
so by Birth or Election, and as to these who have been such by Election even
to their Electors; And at you I inquire, where think you to shelter in the Great
Day of the Lord ? I can not think you are so Mad as to Dream that his Majesties Letter will serve your Turn here. I suppose you know your Privileges
better, that it is due right in conjunction with his Majesty to Enact Laws in
this Realm, and sure when these Laws, against which, I in the strength of my
blessed Master have set my self, came to be enacted, you could not but know
that these same were not only contrary, directly contrary to the Will of God,
your and our Supream Lord and Master, but also contrary to the very many
then and still, standing Laws, (notwithstanding these mock ones of yours to
the contrary) how then durst you in obedience to that Letter do any thing,
or meddle with any Oath that might import either a Resiling from our
greatest Soveraign, or a Counteracting of Laws, by as good, at least, if not bet-

ter,

ter Fellows than your selves? I mean our own Predeceffors who have had more of the Countenance of God one day, than you can with the leaft fhadow of Reafon pretend to thefe twenty two, or twenty three Years.

And for your Electors, have you this to produce for your Vindication that you called the Members by you Elected to an Account for their Maluerfation? If you have not this, I hope I need not tell you, that you muſt cover under the Short and Narrow Mantle of the Kings Letter with the reft; and againſt you and thefe Elected by you, and thefe fitting there by Birth, fhall the relinquiſhing of thefe Parliaments on thefe Terms of both Sorts, not only be a ſtanding Teſtimony, but fhall alfo quite Denude you of your poor fhort and Narrow Mantle, can you Dream or think a Letter from our poor Clay King, can not only Vindicate you from what juſt Refentment you may (in our bleffed Lords time and way) meet with from fucceeding free Parliaments; but alfo from what our Glorious Lord himſelf may juſtly quarrel you with, for fuch grofs affronts againſt the Sacred Majeſty of Heaven in thefe Hellifh Acts, and Actings? I ſay, can ye be ſo mad as to Dream thefe things? If you be, I can affure you, in the bleffed Name of my Bleffed Lord and Maſter, you fhall find but a pitiful and empty Dream.

Next muſt I come to the Sheriffs, Conſtables, Bailies of Burrows and Regalitys with all others under his Majeſty, and free called Parliaments of whatfomer Rank quality or condition, and ask at you where you mind to fhelter in that Day for your Executing of thefe GOD provoking, Soul Deſtroying, Church Confounding, Nation Dividing and only Devil pleafing Acts of theirs? Think ye to Shelter your felves either under thefe Acts themfelves, or the Authority of the Perfon enacting the fame? Know you not that thefe Acts in their full vigour are againſt the Almighty, and have for their tendency next to h s difhonour the confounding of his Church, Oppreffion of his People both as to their Spiritual and Temporal Privileges, and the pleafure of Belzebub only and his Agents? And think you the Authority of thefe pitiful Servants and Deputes will fhelter you from our great LORD himſelf, whofe difpleafure in thefe affairs you could not be ignorant of if it were not wilfully, which will never excufe you, and if you will not believe me, I hope ye will Sir George Mckenzie of Rofehaugh, who fays the fame in his Treatife of Criminals, and fince I have here met with him, I muſt anent him tell you a very fad Story, I being at the Caſtle-hill of Edinburgh upon a Morning with two Commerads, fome 17 or 18 years ago, he and Sir George Lockart and Sir Andrew Birnie, if my Memory ferve me ſtanding by us, looking upon fome Companies of Foot who were Marching down the Long Gate to Leith Links, who were Levied a litile after the Reintroduction of the Horrid Prelates, I heard him diſtinctly ſay, the Devil take me if ever I loved the Church that ſtood in need of fuch Ruling Elders as thefe ; I tell this the rather that the Reader with me may the better pafs our Judgment anent this Man, who has oftner than once or twice Raked Hell for Inventions to Vent his Love to that Church, which he feemed then to loath, and his rage againſt our GOD in that Church which he did, at leaſt tacitely then feem to be a favourer of, Well may I ask at this Gentleman if he has Ratified this his fo frank Refignation to the Devil? O is it his ſtruglings in this Matter that Occafions that Horror in his Confcience,

which

which some call Hypocondrick Fitts; others Excercise? If it be a Right Christian Exercise indeed, I pray it may be through; but his so frequent Relapses, gives the more Ground than I desire to fear the contrary.

In the next place, I come to ask at the Soldiers of a lower degree, for with the Officers I have met already, and what I have said to one, I expect they will be so favourable to themselves, as to look upon said to all, unless they have some particular Exceptions that I know not of, the benefite of which I allow them, desiring them rather to err in judging of themselves too much than too little. And to you Soldiers I say, where think you to shelter your selves in the great Day of our LORD? Do ye Dream to shelter your selves under the Command of your Supream Officers? If so, I think you have a very pitiful Plea, for in the first place, hereby you denude your selves of the priviledge due to all Rational Creatures (I mean of your Discretive Judgment) and in the next place, the commands of all created Powers, is only in so far a Warrand to the Observant as that command Quadrats and agrees with the will of our Supream Lord and Master, which I affirm still to be the Supream Law: Now where are you Poor things, if these Commands you have been obeying be Diametrically opposite to the Supream Law, I mean the revealed will of our Supream Lawgiver, which none who duely ponders what is here written, with what is contained in the abovementioned Authors, will easily get refused, if this hold as surely it must for any thing we have heard to the contrary, then you are still to seek for a shelter, for your Officers Commands will no more secure you, than their Superiors did them, which is not at all as you may see above, and I hope yet more afterward. For my own part, I must here Vent my Opinion which is, I look upon no more as Lawfull but what is purely Defensive, neither do I think, the War gets the Denomination of Offensive or Defensive, from the Priority or Posteriority of Parties contending in their Assaults, or infalls upon one another, so much as upon the Equity or Iniquity of the ground of the Quarrel, he upon whose side Equity stands, being still Defender, and the other Offender, and this in all the Revolutions of the War, to the end, whoever pursue, whoever fly, whoever give the first, whoever give the second blow, (I mean with the Sword) for the War with me is determined as to its nature er'e it come to blows if it begin not by a blow, which seldom falls out. And now I hope my Lord *Boyd*, as I remember, is satisfied as to that Curious Question proponed by him to me by another, who (if I remember right was Mr. *David Thores*, Advocate) in the Outter House, when I was Overseeing the Writing of my Subscribed Declaration, proposed the same, which was, If the Infall upon *Glasgow* was in self Defence? I am sure it was, however pitifully managed by some there.

And now in the last Place (fearing I have been too Tedious already) I must Adress my self to a Mixt Multitude some upon one Account, some upon another, who may Possibly think they have not been so Active as the Rest, as being as but they call it Passive in the thing, if the Enacters and others above Spoken to have been Guilty in their Activity, Dream not of Escaping under that Feg Tree Leaf of Passive Obedience a Perfect Chimera (in the matter of Sin) for there is nothing will Justify Sin, whether Committed Active or Passive, and to call a Mans Sufferings for not Sinning Passive Obedience is to make use of an Unproper

Speech

Speech, for it is indeed Difobedience and Suffering for the fame, and to Dream thefe have been Simply Paffive, to whom I am to Addrefs my felf, becaufe their Practice is Warranted by a Human Law, their Tranfgreffion being againft the Almighty GOD *Jehovah*, yet more Unproper. You fhall know the Perfons I intend here are fuch Mafters of Ground in the Country, as for fear of Mens Laws have Refufed our Bleffed Lord, fo much of their Ground as to meet with his People in for Preaching and Praying, and the Reft of the Duties of Publick Worfhip, though the Earth be the Lords and the Fullnefs thereof, then fuch Mafters of Houfes, whether in Burgh or Landwart, as Refufe the Poor People of GOD, either Shelter, Meat or Drink, then fuch as Concur with our more Active Enemies in putting us in Prifon, Convoying us to Scaffolds, meeting us in Crofs ways, looking upon us with Satisfaction in the Day of Diftrefs, and Refufing for fear to Vifit us in our Diftrefs as they are called (but Bleffed be the Lord, many of his Poor People have found them among their Chiefeft Enlargements) fuch I fay, as are Guilty of thefe and many others of that Nature, thefe being Sirs, all againft GOD, as you may fee on the Margine of the Scriptures Cited there, the Committing thereof, can neither be Excufed by the Commands or Laws of Men, nor by that Diftinction of Paffive Obedience, which I faid in the matter of Sin is a Meer Chimera, becaufe I had this Paffive Obedience offered to me by Sir *John Lauder*, whom I did not know then to be Sir *John*, and therefore called him only Mr. *Lauder*, for which I hope he will readily Excufe me my Ignorance. Being in fome fort Invincible, I fhall firft give an Account of that meeting and what paft there, then Endeavouring to Satisfy Sir *John* in that matter, and afterward Return to the Perfons I have in hand, fome three or four Days before my Efcape being called down, I knew not to whom nor for what End, till I was Convoyed by one of the Keepers unto a little Room in the Hall, where I fees Sir *John* and another Gentleman, whom I knew not then, but Underftands fince to have been a Brother of the Juftice Clerks, *Andrew Young* Writer to the Signet, Mr. *John Vafs* one of the Keepers, and another Gentleman, whom I knew neither then nor could learn fince; when I came in, Sir *John Lauder* Saluted me, telling me, that partly out of Refpect to my Father, his Father, and mine being Old Accquaintance, and partly out of Refpect to my felf, he had come to Pay me a Vifite, I told him there was no Civil Gentleman but fhould be Welcome to Vifite me, then they defired me to Sit down, I am no fooner Sit down, than Sir *John* tells me he did Compaffionate my Condition, I told him I was not fenfible of any thing in my Condition that called for his Compaffion (for which I Bleffed then, and I hope fhall ever Blefs my GOD) he fays, why are you fo Tenacious in the matter of Defenfive Arms? I told him I had for me, in that, not only the Example of *Abraham* the Father of the Faithful, but which was yet more two Precepts by my Bleffed Lord and Mafter Jefus Chrift, the one that, *Sell your Coat and buy a Sword*, the other that, *when you are Perfecute out of one City Fly to another*, and befides all thefe, the Law of Nature, the Law of Nations Generaly and Particularlly, our own and the Practice of all our Reformed Churches both at Home and Abroad : All thefe he paft, and Touches at that, *Sell your Coat and buy a Sword*, fo foon as he Mentioned this, I defired him to beware of the Rock, Sir *William Paterfon*, in calling the Sword

there

to all Chriftains to make ufe of the fame, in their own innocent felf Defence to the Worlds end. Then fayes Mr. *John Vafs*, Mr *Dick* you know the word *Buy* is varioufly taken in Scripture, fometimes Figuratively as in that of *Ifai: Buy Wine and Milk, &c.* I told him, I knew that, but durft he or any elfe fay, it was taken fo in the place under Debate ? Adding, could there be any thing more clear or lefs Figurative then Sell your Coat, and as if he had faid with the price thereof Buy a Sword, Infinuating that after hisDeparture they fhould have more need of Swords then Cloaths. Mr. *Vafs* was offering fomewhat elfe, which I hindered by Charging him to beware of doing Violence to the Spirit of GOD, which when I was faying, I gave a Moderate chop upon the Table ; For which I could not pafs without *Andrew Toungs* Check, that I was of a too fiery Spirit. To which I Anfwered, I knew I had a Natural Infirmity in that, but that the Lord had helped me in fome Meafure to ftrive againft it, gave me no fmall Satisfaction : I told them alfo, thefe Swords our Bleffed Lord gave Commiffion to Buy were either for offence, Defence, or both (of which above) to this I got no Anfwer ; Only I Remember Sir *John Lauder* told me fomewhat of *Paffive Obedience*, and Inftanced *Tertullian* anent it, what it was I Totally Difremember. But what ever it were, I muft tell Sir *John* once for all, that fuffering fimply comes under no Divine Precept, and whatever he have elfe for it, I matter the lefs, fince I have my Bleffed Mafters Precept for *Active Refiftance*, Innocent felf Defence, this Serves me, and if he tell me I ought rather to fuffer then Sin, I fhall readily grant it, and yet in that give no *Paffive Obedience*, but fuffer for Difobedience. But of this enough confidering what is upon this head, contained in the abovementioned Authors, particularly *Jus Populi*.

Now thereafter, That modeft and moderate Gentleman, I fuppofe his Name be Sir *John Maitland*, told me very meekly, he was very glad I had been interrupted in oppofing my felf to the Laws of the Land in which I was a Subject, leaft my cafe fhould have been worfe. I Anfwered him with as much meeknefs as my hot fpurred Nature was capable of, I knew no Laws I had oppofed, which were not Diametrically oppofite to the exprefs Texts of Scripture, which I judged neither I, nor any other Chriftian was obliged to own for Laws, and that I had been hindered for to Defend my felf from the Word of GOD, and had gotten it denyed me by the Juftice Clerk, that the fame was the Supream Law, I judged a very great Injuftice, for which they were all to Anfwer to GOD, with whom I knew that was ftanding on Record. The Gentlemen faid nothing, but Sir *John Lauder* would have refufed this, but I told him, chaping yet more eagerly u n the Table, What Sir ? Ye refufe me, that for which I have no fewer tha Five Hundred Witneffes, and which is yet more, I am fure it ftands Regiftrate in Heaven.   Now

Now to return where we left, to the Landlords in Landward and Towns, to these Convoyers to Prisons and Scaffolds and others we have elaffed with you, What are you refolved to do in that great and terrible Day of our Lord? Think not to fhelter under thefe Laws, for the very Inactors themfelves as you have heard, fhall be as far to feek as to fhelter as you, nor ever dream, that your Lands and Houfes for prefervation whereof you have finned againft my great Mafter, fhall hear you when ye cry upon them, to hide you, may ye not expect fuch an Anfwer from them as this? Do you not remember how long not only we but the whole Creation groaned under the burden of your Sins? As you Anfwered our Groans, then fo fhall we Anfwer you now. Confider then Friends in time, where you will fhelter, and what will you do in that day.

But now to come yet nearer you all in Bulk, let us make yet another Effay, for though I can not fay with *Paul, that I would be content to be Accurfed for my Brethren*, nor yet with *Mofes, Let my Name be Bloted out of the Book of Life*; Yet I affure you my heart Yearns for my Acceptation of this my Fecklefs endeavour, and for a Bleffing from my GOD to it; it may be it has been in Mercy to not a few, that GOD has put thefe things into my heart, and I may fay has had the Patience by his Spirit, to Dictate thefe things to me, and if any of you reap Profite thereby; I obteft you to return the whole Praife to my Bleffed Lord and Mafter. Then to you all *in cumulo*, let me again propofe this Queftion, what are you Refolved upon? Are you yet undetermined? Will ye not follow my fimple Honeft hearted Advice? Or will you not apply your felves to our Honeft Minifters up and down the Nations, both Old and Young for Council, whofe it is more properly to deall in this Affair? I fay will ye not hear me in thefe things? And do you not for all that is faid in the Word of God, nor that you have heard of others, nor from what you have heard from me your Poor Friend, believe that there is a God, that there is a Hell, that there is a Heaven, that there is a day of Judgement coming? I would fain hope it is not fo with you; for in this you fhould be worfe as to your cafe and condition, nor are the very Devils themfelves, for they believe all thefe things and Trimble. And yet indeed it would be matter of comfort to us to know, that fome of you were come this length, though we hope better things of others, Believe, Believe Dear Friends what we are telling you from that Unerring Word of GOD, our Supream Law, leaft you be forced Untimoufly fo to do, which yet will be fo much the fadder unto y u, if you Reject this my Friendly Advice.

I fay again unto you all, What refolve you to do in that Great and Terrible Day of the LORD? When Our Bleffed Lord Jefus Chrift the Lamb of GOD, for Meeknefs and Pleafantnefs to His People, but to all who fhall be found Enemies in that Day, The Lyon of the Tribe of *Judah*, and a very Terrible Lyon fhalt he be. What are you refolved to do? Can it be poffible, that Men who were created reafonable Creatures can have fallen upon fo Defperate a Cure as this, I mean as to have Unanimoufly Refolved (upon the firft hearing of the Trumpet that day) to Loup quick into Hell, and there to hide themfelves?

Sure if this be the thing intended it fhall not only be a Defperately, Mad but ineffectual Refolution alfo. What? Do you not know that thence alfo the Omnipotent Arm of *Jehovah* fhall eafily bring you out? Dream not I fay, Dream

not

...hortation and Advice I must here warn you before him to make ready, to answer for all you have done in the Flesh, and though to some of you the flighting of this my Advice may be the last; Yet it shall not be the least of the Challenges you shall meet with this day. Now I hope I have prevailed with the most part, if not all of you to Believe, that before this Lyon you must come and look him in the Face also, and before him answer for what you have done in the flesh, and having told you who is to be your Judge, for your further fitting for that Rancounter I shall also tell you by what Law you are to be Judged, even by the written Word of GOD, wherein is contained our Blessed LORD's revealed Will, that self same Law that you refuse to be supream, and when my Companion in Tribulation and fellow Sufferer for Christ Jesus *George Lapsly* called it the Acts of Parliament of Heaven pertinently enough, yet some of your Number in rage against our great Law maker Disdainfully did Laugh, I say by this self same Law are you all and every one of you to be Judged: And however you may be so Diabolically bold, as to Contemn it now, you shall not then dare to whisper in the least against it. Now having told who is to be Judges, and what the Law by which you are to be Judged, if you incline to know who are to be Witnesses, we tell you even your own Consciences with that great Book of Remembrance, the comparing of which together shall be as sufficient as Millions of Witnesses: Then for your Assizers, know you are to have the whole Generation of the Righteous, and amongst the rest, even these whom you in your rage against the Almighty have slain for the Testimony of our blessed Lord and Master Christ Jesus, whom you have not only Renounced your selves (as Head of his Church) but also are raging in madness against all such as will not run with you run into the same excess of Riot. The Dyet of your Compearance we have told you before.

And now again I Obtest and Charge you, as you shall Answer to the ever Living GOD, that you either grant me my former Freindly Request and Christian Exhortation, or otherwise make you ready to stand Naked and Bare before this our ever Blessed Judge, and there to be in Readiness as to Answer for all you have done in the Flesh in General, so to this our Particular Charge following, to which we would very Gladly know what you shall be able to Answer. Now again I Charge you all from the Highest to the Lowest, that you (Staging your selves in the Sight of our Blessed Lord, whom to your Sad Experience you shall find in that Day to be to you a Lyon indeed) may make ready to Answer these following Queries, wherein ye ule you are all Equally truly concerned, though there be amongst you as to them some Gradual Difference, we are to Pose you all in *Cumulo*, being Resolved in the Lords

Strength

Strength to Touch more Particularly, at the Perfons more Particularly concerned in the feveral Queſtions. And firſt, what will you Anſwer for that Unparalelled Act of Rebellion againſt *Jehovah*? I mean your Overturning the whole Work of Reformation, that fo very Glorious Work, and fo Correſpondent to the Revealed will of GOD, as that Excerciſed and Practiſed by our Bleſſ'd LORD himſelf, and his Holy Apoſtles, and all the feveral Churches their Succeſſors for not a few Hundreds of Years after them, as is clear from the Word of GOD and the Writings of our Divines founded thereon, to which till this Hour, we have never feen nor Heard of any thing looking like a Satisfactory Anſwer ; and this over the Belly of a moſt Solemn Covenant, to the Obſervance whereof every individual Soul of you ſtands yet firmly Obliged (and I am ſure you muſt give me leave to fay fo, when you conſider you Refuſed me an Anſwer to the Queſtion, by what Authority are theſe Covenants Infringed or Loofed?) And ſhall be while Sun and Muon Endures: And not only fo but in the Room hereof, Introducing that Abominable and GOD Diſpleaſing Prelacy, a Weed which our Bleſſed LORD never Planted, yea which he was at no fmall Pains, while in time to Guard his Diſciples againſt, in his feveral Exhortations to Study Humility and forbear Lording over their Brethren, and over the LORD's Inheritance, and feveral others to this Purpoſe, as alſo his briſk Checks for any think of this Nature that offered to fet up tis head in his Bleſſed time, with his own Bleſſed Example, in Girding himſelf with a Towel and Waſhing his Diſciples Feet, in which you are yet the more Inexcuſable, that by the fame Covenant, this Abominable Weed is forever thrown over the Hedges of the true Churches of *Britain* and *Ireland*, I mean theſe Presbyterian ; I fay what will you Anſwer for theſe things, when before the Son of GOD that Day? And further what will you yet Anſwer, for not only Practiſing fo your felves, but alſo by Armed Force, Compelling the Reſt of the Nations to Concur with you in this fo Abominable Combination and Rebellion againſt *Jehovah*? (of wich above) what will you Anſwer, I fay? Do you think that Blaſphemous Maxim of your's (no Biſhop no King) will Serve your turn? No fure, it will not. May ye not Expect a Severe Check from your Judge for that, when he ſhall tell you firſt, that it is Expreſly Contrary to his Revealed will ? 2dly. That it is the fame upon the matter with that Proponed by the Jews themſelves, to his ever Bleſſed felf in faying the owners of our Bleſſed LORD and Maſter, were no Friends to *Ceſar*, or does our King think to Anſwer he was Counſelled thereto will do his turn? No fure he can not be fo Mad. And what can theſe his Counſellors fay ? Sure nothing; this I am the rather to Believe, that I find none of them have any thing to Anſwer here and Sure much lefs there.

My fecond Queſtion is, what will you anſwer to our ever bleſſed Lord and Maſter your Judge, when that Queſtion is propoſed to the King, how came it Sir that you were fo inſolently bold and daring, as to Strive with me for State ? And though my ever bleſſed Father bequeathed that upon me as one of my Royal Prerogatives to be King and Head of all my Churches, which as I was to lead and guide by my Spirit in their inviſible Capacity, fo by my Spirit in my Servants (according to my Commiſſion to them) in their viſible Capacity, for which theſe my Servants were to me only to anſwer, and I

having

having for their better encouragement and more diftinct management of thefe their affairs, left it on Record that the Spirits of the Prophets were fubiect to the Prophets, fo that my Churches in themfelves in the feveral Nations were Judicatories totally feparate in their Nature, and diftinct from the Civil, they being fpiritual, and for which they as to their behaviour were only anfwerable to me as Kings and other Judges were for their carriage in Civil, (this you have fully made out in the abovementioned Authors, and others our Divines as you may fee in their Treatifes) what will our King have to anfwer for himfelf here ? I am fure he will ftand Mute, as will all thefe who have Combined with him in this their rage againft the Almighty, in not only fetting him upon our bleffed Lords Chair (over Mala part) but alfo declairing this a Privilege Inherent to the Crown.

My third queftion fhall be next ? What will one and all of you anfwer for Impofing in fuch a violent manner that horrid and Monftrous Oath, the *Teft* upon the Subjects of this Nation, anent which by and attour the Nonfenfe and contradictions I have Hinted before, you may from the Pen of a more Solid Judicious and Reverend Author, learn yet more of the Abominations thereof, (which if it be not come to your Hands already, I hope yet may come fhortly in a fmall Treatife againft the Hearing of thefe Soul-Murdering *Curats*)I fay, what will you anfwer to your Judge in that day for this? can it be poffible that thefe Monftrous *Curats* with the reft of their curfed Clergy can think to fhelter in that Mock Qualification they got added, that the Oath to them is Reftricted to the King's power in externals ? Now can thefe infrabrutal wretches think that a Qualification made pofterior to, and not contained in the Body of the Oath (in which they Swear exprefly to take the Oath in its true genuine Meaning, without equivocation or mental refervation) can do their turn here ; and though it were contained in their Oath, the Claufe being general ? And who knows not that *fraus latet in generalibus*, which no Man of Confcience durft ever Venture upon in the Matter of an Oath ? And fure I am the fenfe of this his Majefty's power in externals could be no Unknown thing to them who know that the Practice of the Law Makers is the beft Commentate upon the general Claufes in their Laws, they can not but know that his Majefty, his Council, and other Civil Judicatories meddle in the Examination of Minifters, Doctrine, out putting and in putting of Minifters and feveral others, which time and the Nature of this my Teftimony will not allow me to enumerate : And this *Prima inftantia* ; I am fure none who are not willfully Blind, will call thefe Externals anent which I recommend the Reader the abovementioned Authors, I fay again what fhall you all anfwer to thefe things ?

My Fourth Queftion is, what will you Anfwer that Day to your Judge, for Preffing by Armed Force the Chriftians in *Britain* and *Ireland*, to joyn in hearing with thefe Abominable Mifcreants your Prelats, and their Underlings in making of and Fighting againft GOD, in that Mock Worfhip of their's, when you fhall know that not only they be none of GOD's Appointing, but againft that Peoples Joyning with whom the Covenants made in thefe Nations with the Almighty ftands yet Binding, by which the People of GOD there are Bound, not only not to Joine with them but to Endeavour in their

feveseveral Capacities and Stations, to use their Uonmost Endeavour for their Extirpation, and if to all this you add this Consideration, that having Renounced Christ for their head, they have set up his Profest and Avowed Enemy (by them others of their Kidney Instigate to be so) in his Room, may ye not conceive, that beside the former Bars in the Lords Peoples way, Whereby they are Deterred from this Practice, this may have no small Influence; that a Tender Hearted Christian may be under such an Impression, that to Join with such under the Notion of Christians as have Renounced Christ for their head, may Involve them in that Fault called by Logicians Repugnantia in Adjecto, and by us Scots Men Downright Nonsence, and a Flet Contradiction, and indeed to me a Christian Disclaiming Christ for his head is Flat Nonsense; Now I say what will you Answer for that so Horrid Practice? I hope if you will be at Pains to Read what has been Written by severals upon this head, you will not only find the Refusers in this Justifiable; but that your Pressing the same with so much Vigour, is of a Peice with the Rest of your Fightings against our Blessed LORD.

My Fifth Question is, what do you one and all of you Resolve to Answer, when our Blessed LORD and Master your Judge shall make Inquisition for all the Innocent Blood has been by you Shed, whither in Fields or upon Scaffolds, or by drowning or whatsomever manner of way? And to begin with the Eminently Worthy Nobleman the Late Marquis of Argyle against whom, though your Invention Raked Hell for a Clock to cover it; yet to all Unbyassed Spectators, it is more then Evident, that your great, if not only Quarrel was, his Befreinding the Cause of Christ; and Precious Eminently worthy and Reverend Mr. James Guthrie, whom in your Rage against the Almighty you Murdered for no other Cause, but his Asserting Christ to be head over the Church, in Refusing to Answer any of your Courts which were not of his and our Masters Appointment, in Matters Spritual and Ecclesiastical Prima Instantia, and all the Rest from these to mine, which you are as really called to Charge your selves with, as if you had been Permitted to put in Execution, that Abominable Unjust Sentence, of yours Pronounced against a Christian, offering to Justify all his Principles and Practises from the Word of GOD, and Requiring no more at your hands for that End, but that ye would grant him the Almighty to be the Supream Judge and his Word the Supream Law, which both were Refused in that the Latter was not Granted, and yet both by my Blessed Lord and Master in my Escape proven.

The first in this that though the Great ones in the Earth Had Decreed my Death upon the 26 of Sept. 1683; yet now see my blessed Master having Decreed the contrary has proven himself Supream. The latter in this, that though the same was Enacted in a Law by you, yet by his Word which is yet the Supream Law, my GOD having moved me to cast mine Eye upon that Promise, *He that loseth his Life for my sake shall save it*, and upon the back of this on that Word in the Psalms, *According to thy Righteousness do thou deliver me*, I say my blessed Lord helping me to cast mine Eye, and not a little to Confide in the Promise, (though I must confess by my too eager gripping thereto at first, and in so doing limitting my blessed Lord) I Bred my self not a little Disquiet, yet I say my

Lord

Lord according to this his Word, having set me at Liberty though you had Enacted the contrary has *ad hominem* sufficiently proven my second Principle also. I say are you at a Point what to answer, when all this Blood comes to .be inquired into? Know you not that the Blood of Saints is precious in the Lord's fight? Or will ye yet with. *Pharaoh* harden your hearts, possibly under this confideration, that you live Remote from the Red-Sea? But know you not that our Omnipotent Mafter can for you make a Sea of your own Blood, if it be Red enough for you to Drown in? And who knows but fuch a thing may come to pafs? Especially confidering, that it is an ordinary thing with the Lord in punifhing either Friends or Enemies to do it fo as their fin may be Read in their Judgement, and I am indeed the rather inclined to think it fhall be fo, when I remember the faying of that Worthy Man of GOD, I mean Mr. *Semple*, late Minifter of *Corsfairn* in *Galloway* (who fell under no fmall Eclipfe in his Latter Days through his clofing with that fatall Indulgence, fatall indeed to the poor Churches in *Britain* and *Ireland*) who in his better days had this Expreflion, As the Lord lives, for every Drop of the Saints Blood has been or ✗ fhall be fhed by thefe his Cruel Enemies (fpeaking of the Malignant, Prelati-cal, Papiftical and Atheiftical Party in thefe Kingdoms) there fhall Tuns Tuns Tuns of their's fall to the Ground, and I know few of this Great Seer Threat-nings have fallen to the Ground; What Dream you I fay you fhall have to An-fwer in that Day? Dare ye whifper thefe things were done conform to your Laws (which upon the Matter was all I got anfwered to me ftanding at your Bar here upon Earth, for which I have no fewer than 500 Witnefles, and upon which I have an Inftrument ftanding Recorded in Heaven) do you think you will dare to Mutter this then? Sure if you knew what you were faying you would never do it here nor there, for it is no lefs upon the Matter than to Ratifie the Sentence paft upon our blefled Lord and Mafter himfelf by the Jews, for which he got no other reafon but we have a Law (the fame I get) but what if our blefled Lord your Judge fay, but you know I had a Law to the contrary, and your Law fhould have Ceded to mine, dare you think you fhall contradict this there, as you have indeed done here upon Earth? I know you dare not, confider then what you will anfwer, for I can affure you it is of your Concern.

May Sixth Queftion fhall be, what think you to Anfwer for your Mock Thankfgivings, of which I fhall Inftance two, one is for *Gowries* Confpiracy, the other for this Pretended Deliverance from a Mock Plot, thefe two Twins I bring in together, the rather that they refemble other as much as ever Twins did, and no wonder fince they are of one Father, I mean the Devil, one Mo-ther the Pope of *Rome*, one Nurfe the Jefuitical Papifts who having brought up thefe Brats till they are able to walk alone, fend them over here to their Friends in *Britain* and *Ireland*, and what day is pitched upon here for bring-ing them forth to publick View? Even the Lords day, in which thefe young Monfters muft get on all their Gay Cloathes, and of them muft all the Churches in the Nations fpend that day in fpeaking (though to the mocking of GOD with abominable Lies yet) to the admiration of this Monftrous Birth; And when all is done there muft be Bonefires, Ringing of Bells, and fireing of
Cannons

Cannons and what not, that this Monſtrous Generation can deviſe for provocking of and fighting againſt Jehovah! O Heaven ſhake, Earth tremble, and all fleſh be aſtoniſhed at ſuch Helliſh madding againſt our glorious Maſter, and becauſe *contravia juxta ſe poſita clarius elucefcunt*, I would have you to take a glance of the induſtrie of that Limb of Antichriſt the Duke of *Iork* in hindering the procedure of the Parliament of *England*, in their ſo juſt and Legall procedure, in inquiring into that Hell-hatched Popiſh Plot, which is in no ſmall meaſure now advanced by this laſt mock one of yours; And I am ſure none who are not altogether Strangers to the Conſtitutions of *England* will refuſe that Treaſon of the Nature that a Popiſh Plot is really, and this mock-Plot of theirs as to its pretended Nature, is pretended to be ought to come under Tryal by his Majeſty and the two Houſes of Parliament, as only competent Judges thereto, but there is no remedy for open and irreſiſtible violence but patience I ſay, what? are you at a Point, what to Anſwer for theſe things? I fear not, and I hope none who knows that I am a Presbyterian, and Conſequently whom I am concerned to Defend here, I mean all ſuch as are either indeed Presbyterians, or longing for the time when the Nation ſhall be Univerſaly ſuch (which the LORD haſten and Pardon, any who have been any way Inſtrumental in hindering, when the matter was brought to a very hopefull paſs) will think I have been out of the Road, in medling in matters, wherein the Glory of GOD is ſo much concerned, for to Charge any ſuch Plotts upon ſuch as are indeed of our Principles, I dare Averr to be not only a wrong for us, but of our Bleſſed LORD alſo in and though us. Now I Pray you conſider what you ſhall Anſwer for theſe things.

My Seventh Queſtion is, what you think to Anſwer, who have Refuſed our Bleſſed LORD and his People, a Spot of your Ground to meet together upon, who have Refuſed his People a Nights Lodging, who have Concurred in Dragging his People to Scaffolds and Priſons, and others whom we have Claſſed together with you above, when you ſhall meet that Day with your Particular Charges? Is it not of your concern to conſider this, eſpecialy the rather that ſuch of you as have Sworn the *Teſt*, have as I Remember in the 15. Article of the Confeſſion of Faith, you have Sworn to therein Declared it to be a Good Work, to Releive the Oppreſt Defend and Patronize the Harmleſs, I ſay, ſo much the rather that your preſent practice and that your Oath Claſhes together, are you not concerned to know what you will Anſwer in that Day? And indeed for my part, I can conceive no Anſwer you or any of you can have to theſe or any of theſe things, therefore I yet Obteſt you to take my Freindly Warning. Now Dare I Flattter my ſelf ſo far as to think that I have got any of you that Length as to Speir, what ſhall we do? (And Oh that I were ſo) however I ſhall out of Tenderneſs to the Glory of GOD, the Good of your Souls, and the well being of theſe Nations, and the well of your Poſterity Adventure in the Strength of my Bleſſed LORD, to Adviſe you as follows.

And firſt Great Sir, be Intreated to lay aſide your Enmity at my Great Lord and Maſter, and you under him to whom together with his Majeſty, I Addreſs my ſelf; Be intreated, and I obteſt you in the Name of GOD ſo to do, and to concur with me in Adviſing his Majeſty thus with me, and as that in Teſtimony

of

of your doing fo : His Majefty with your Advice and Confent, would call a free Parliament in his feveral Dominions, which may meet without either Prelimitations or Reftrictions, in which let the firft Act be the Appointment of a Faft, to be keeped for many days, by all the Faithfull Minifters Living in thefe Kingdoms, who have been fo much Difcountenanced, to the Difhonour of GOD thefe 22 or 23 Years, till the Performance of which can be ended. Let this your Parliament be Adjourned, then let your next Work be to Empty, all the Prifons in the three Kingdoms, of all the Honeft Chriftians you have in Prifon there, for no other reafon, then that they are fuch. And in the next place in their Room, let thefe prifons be filled with all that have given his Majefty unfaithfull Council fince his Reftauration as formerly, beginning with his Brother the Duke of *York*, and fo from him, to all the reft in order, forget not the *Prelates*, and fuch of their Underlings, as have been too too Active, in driving on thefe Defections, and that Damnable *Apoftacy*, and as to their Treafonable Practices, let them all be brought and Arraigned before thefe Parliaments; Then let there be an Act Emitted for the *Presbyterian* Minifters in the feveral Nations, to meet in a General Affembly, for confidering, what may be the moft effectuall courfe, for fettling the Churches in thefe Nations, and for Removing thefe Abominations and Abufes, that have been introduced through want of the Hedge (and over the Belly of Covenants, Sworn to the Almighty, ftanding ftill in Vigour) to the great Difhonour of GOD, and Utter Confufion of thefe Nations, both as to Church and State. If I get but thefe granted, I hope it fhould be a very good beginning, and bad Councils being once removed, and better brought in their Room, with Dependance on the Almighty for a Bleffing, I doubt not would eafe me of the Travell of further Counciling, for which I am fenfible of my own infufficiency, and yet I think this I have given none of the worft, and I can affure one, and all of you in following the fame, you fhall not only do GOD good Service but your felves alfo, and thefe Nations, and your Pofterity.: It's like fome may think my advice here is the lefs folid, that I advife fome to act againft themfelves, and fome near Relations to act againft on another; But I hope fuch fhall eafily alter their opinion, when they confider, that fometimes it is better for the Body to have fome of the Members cut off, then to have all indangered together; And though amongft Naturalifts for perfons to act feemingly, contrary to themfelves, may not found fo well, yet I hope amongft Divines it may; who know it is no Difparragement to the beft of Mortalls to come in time to our Bleffed LORD with the Rope about their Neck and acknowledge their Guilt, Submitting themfelves to his holy Majefty for what of Punifhment he fhall fee fit to inflict. And as I advife his Majefty to do this in time, as the beft Council I can give him, fo do I advife all under him to do the fame; And not only fo, but as a Teftimony of their Stupendious Loyalty they Crack fo much of to our King, that they would now come and give a proof thereof, in coming to his Majefty and this free Parliament, to offer themfelves to Tryall. Sure I am, if they be confiftent with their principals, they are bound in Duty to do this, and I know nothing they can object to the contrary, that will not abundantly more ferve our turn, in our prefent cafe, and come there when they like, I am confident they fhall never find Judges nor Advocats, under fuch a Conftitution, as to grounds and reafons for their Procedure, as we have found there in our cafes.

I make no doubt but that they shall get it made out to their own conviction, that they have one and all of them been not only most Horrid Traitors and Rebells against the Majesty of Heaven, but even against our own King also, and that these have been likewise guilty not only of all the Bloodshed since his Majesties Restauration, but also since that of righteous *Abel* even to this Hour, I mean here the Bloodshed of the Righteous. Now having in some measure remov-ed what might be objected against my Advice I shall leave you to consider, whether you will embrace it or not, and I dare here confidently averr there was no more intended by the Presbyterians in *Scotland* in these two risings at *Pentland* and *Bothwell* than this, or something of this Nature, (our doing the same in Arms being constrained from that Monstrous Act, Discharging any such Addres un-der the pain of Treason) and though I have not much hopes to prevail with you, yet I doubt not but herein I have been in my duty, and who knows but in part even for this end my GOD has set me at Liberty to tell you, what you would not Suffer me to Speak when standing at the Bar before you ? The hearing and Embracing of this my Advise, I am sure should be so far from prejudging any of you, that I doubt not but the Embracers (if any such shall be) shall have our GOD to Bless for it, and for the Refusers that shall yet still with *Pharoh* harden their Necks in Rebellion against my Blessed LORD and Master, I can Assure them from our Unerring Law, the Word of GOD that they shall not have Ground to Crack of it, but that thereby their Judgement shall not only be more certainly Entailed upon them and their posterity, but also (I doubt not) even the former also, for indeed I think our Blessed LORD is saying nothing less by these Dispensations then this, what will not these Stupendious Rebles come and hear Honest Ministers, who are ready and willing to give them Warning, that their Mouths may be for ever Stopped, he'll send them a Warning another way, which if they will Refuse then have at them, so then I come to my last Task with you the Enemies of our GOD and our's upon his Account, and it is to take Instruments upon all my Blessed Master has in and by me the Feeblest of his Servants, been doing with you in all my Tryals as follows.

Most Holy and Infinitly Glorious GOD, the Father of my Blessed Lord Jesus Christ, and my Father in and throw him, I earnistly beg of thee, for thy great Names Sake, for thy Glorys Sake, for the Son of thy Loves Sake, and for the love thou bears to thy poor people in these Nations, that what thou has in thy infinite Wisdome been doing in by and throw me, to and with these thine Enemies, be keept written in large Characters, in the Book of Rememberance, till the great Day of the Lord for a Testimony, and Witnes against all such of them, as shall Contemptously refuse what I thy poor servant has been helped of thee with an Eye to thy Glory, the good of thy people, the Conviction of these thine Enemies, and even the good of the Souls of such of them, as shall give ear to what from thy word, I have in thy strength offered.

And now again, to you stiff Necked Rebeles, against my ever Blessed Lord and Master, may I in the strength of my God, intimate what you are to expect for your small Sentence in the Great Day (if you continue in this your Rebellion) even this which you will find written in the 25 Chapter of *Matthew*, 41 Verse.

I

I lay depart from me ye Curfed into everlasting Fire prepared for the Devil and and his Angels? and of the Reasons there and elsewhere in the Lords Word given for this your Sentence, you have ground to expect your carriage to the rest of the Lords People and me amongst them, shall not be the least afflicting and astonishing to you.

Now having ended with our blessed Lords Enemies I come to my last Task in this my Testimony; which is to speak a short word by way of Advice and Exhortation to all my precious Friends, under which Compellation I comprehend all that love our Lord Jesus Christ and wait for his coming, all that have given themselves to him in a Covenant never to be forgotten, all that are keeping up the Fight against their Corruptions, and Strugling in the Strength of our Lord against a Body of Death, and in short all that are sincerely Arting Heavenward, whither such as are farder or shorter way advanced in their Journey, and to these and all such of whatsomever Nation, Countrey, Tongue or Language they be, whither at Home or Abroad, of whatsomever perswasion consistent with the Foundations of Religion : And particularly to all under the Cross, whither Abroad in *Hungary, France, Germany*, or any other elsewhere, who are in the Furnace, or at Home in these three Kingdoms, and to you all and every one who in the Strength of our blessed Lord shall be helped to run that Race with patience, and finish your Christian Course with Joy. I hope I need not use Arguments to prove, that the day of the Lord which we have been speaking of, above which to the Wicked and to the Enemies of our blessed Lord shall be so terrible, shall be to you the beginning of days, or rather the beginning of a day which is never to have an end, and that this day may be the more Joyful to one and all of us, I shall obtest you all to join with me in the pursuance of these few Christian Exhortations following.

And first in general, let there be a cordial endeavour in the Strength of our blessed Master (the more this be imployed the better speed shall we come) as to strive against every Sin without exception, so to close with every Commanded Duty with delight, the more Universal we be in either the more sincere in our Resolutions this way, the more dependantly upon Christ Jesus we go on in this Course, and the more self denial and denial to all other Airths we be blessed of the Lord with, the better speed surely shall we come.

But secondly and more particularly, let us all Unanimously Concurr in the endeavour after the cordial and sincere performance of these particular Duties following. And first I would offer for your Exercise that indispensible necessary Duty of Repentance, in exercising whereof I shall offer these few Christian Advices, First, Let us Digg deep in this Matter, and never rest till we come to the Root, I mean Original Sin, and after we have Dwelt by Medication upon the sadness thereof, let us in the next place take a View of all our actual Transgressions flowing therefrom, of our Sins as well of Omission as Commission of our Younger as our Riper Age, against the Law as against the Gospel, these sins that thence cleaves to us in our best performances, not forgetting these sins called our own and the sins that do easily beset us, and all these and many others (which you may find out, by perusing great and Reverend Mr. *Durham* upon the Commands) not only as to our selves every one of us for himself, but all of us for each other, and in a special manner be mindful of the publick National sins, and that not only in the Land where you have your Residence, but also all

E   the

the World over ; In sum let every thing done to the Dishonour of GOD by whomsoever, be the Object of your Mourning before him. And I pray forget not these sins whereby our blessed GOD is not only dishonoured; But also the Generation of the Wicked hardened, and the Generation of the Righteous stumbled and offended. I pass their the more generally, that being Interrogate by the Enemies anent a few of them, I was by my blessed Lord determined then to pass it with this Answer, That I judged it no ie of my Duty to publish any thing of that Nature to them, (with an Eye to that Prohibition, *Tell it not in Gath, publish it not in Askelon*) which is indeed the Reason I medle not with these things here, having intended this for publick View, and being resolved in the Lords Strength (either by a distinct Line to the several Parties offending, the like freedom I expect also from them, knowing that in many things not to say in every thing we offend all,) or by laying my self open to what my blessed Lord may offer otherways, to Communicate my Sentiments of these offered whither to these who have gone aside to the Right or Left Hand. 2*dly*, Let us in our Repentings study to have the Dishonour done to our blessed Lord, more weighty upon our Souls than the hazard our Souls lyes under from thence, though we may have an Eye to both, yet let the former very much preponderate. 3*dly*, Let there be much singleness and Heart honesty in the Business. 4*thly*, Let there be much Dependance on the Lord, and prayer for Grace in order to a right Performance.

These and many others (for which I Recomend you to our Faithful Ministers) may be useful in this matter, and for our farder Encouragement in performance of this so very Necessary a Duty, let us consider that the Christian performance thereof, will not only be Refreshful to us in that great day of the LORD, but may be even so also in time, as will be clear to any that will but Read over the 9th. Chapter of *Ezekiel*, and this not from any Vertue of the Duty as proceeding from us but of free Grace, let this be Underltood in Referrence to the Rest of the Duties also.

The Second duty I Propose for the Object of our Sincere Endeavours is the fear and Love of GOD, I bring thir in together the rather that they are Seldom if ever Separate, as it is also with all the other Graces of the Spirit though some of them may be at some times both more or less felt by the party himself, and more or less Visible to others and for our help here, let us Dwell much upon the consideration of that Mystery of Love Vented towards lost Mankind in that Transaction held by the Holy Trinity before the World had a Fundation, I say let the Serious thoughts of that Fountain Love whereby GOD so Loved us, so Loved us that GOD the Father was pleased to want the Refreshfull presence of the Son, and GOD the Son not only to want the most Amiable and Desireable Company of the Father, but also to take upon him our Nature and come down and Dwell amongst us in the World, Rendering himself upon our Account Lyable to all the Miseries of this Li e (Sin only Excepted) even to Death it self and all for us. And GOD the Holy Ghost freely undertaking what was Cut out to him for Task by the Father and Son, in Reference to the further Manifestation of this Mystery of Love, in Applying the Favour so freely Bequeathed on Poor lost Mankind and us amongst the Rest, and sure I am this Seriously Dwelt upon and Prayed over can hardly miss to take effect towards the Warming of our Hearts Godwards, and begetting in our Souls a

Filial

Filial fear of doing any thing to the Dishonour of that Glorious GOD, who so Loved us, and if to this Meditation, we add that of considering the great pains our Blessed GOD has been and is at about us in his Holy Works of Providence, Ordering and Overuling all the Various Revolutions in time, as for his own Glory, so for the Good of the Elect; so that even these Dispensitions that to Poor short Sighted us are looked upon Tending to our Ruine, many times are by that Holy Providence of GOD Ordered for our yet greater Advantage, so that there is no Serious Observer but shall be Forced e're all be done to set to his Seal to the truth of the Scripture, all things shall Work together for Good to them that Love GOD; I say Dwell upon these things till you and I get our Hearts wrought up not only to Cordial Loving of our ever Blessed GOD, but also to a Filial fearing of doing any thing whereby his Glorious Name may be Dishonoured, and for Asistance here let there be much Dependance for the outletting of the Spirit, and if this Love and fear be within it will not Fail to Vent it self in effect, I mean Strenuous Endeavours to live much to the Glory of GOD, upon which I shall desire we lay no other stress then the Probation of these Graces being within.

The Third thing I offer for the Object of our Sincere and Cordial Endeavours is, the Actual Excercise of the Grace, the Noble and Fountain Grace of Faith, as also of Patience, this can also hardly be Separate, since he that Believes makes no haste, I doubt not to say it that I hope there are not a few thousands in *Britain* and *Ireland*, who have these Graces in the Root and Habite, who are too too much Strangers to the Actual-Exercise thereof at this present time, and this is so much the Sadder that there has no Bitt of the short and Evil time, I have had in this World Cryed more Loudly for the same. And do ye not think that our Blessed, even our Blessed LORD may very truly say to us, what he said to others before in our Case, that he can not do many Mighty Works amongst us, because of our Unbeleif: I Doubt nothing but that there are many Christians in *Britain* and *Ireland*, and other Places all the World over that would willingly have our great LORD appearing in their Behalf, why is it then that we look so like a People under a Combination to bind his holy hand (to Speak so with holy Reverence) for though indeed our Faith as it is our Act can not Merite at the Hands of our Blessed LORD that he should appear, yet it being a mean of his Blessed appointment and a Gift of his own giving, whereby in his Holy Providence he Disposes his People, and puts them in Capacity to Receive his Favours, the least we are called to do is to Importunate the Throne of Grace, for the Exercise thereof, and for our Encouragement herein let us not only Read but Seriously consider that 11 Chapter of the *Hebrews*, where we shall meet with a Glorious Company of Believers, and of the special and great Blessings Attending that their Beleif, and with this we have added Patience, that by our Impatient Thristing, even after that which may be the Object of our Faith, we do not Marr the Work with our own Hands, and though our Blessed LORD as to his comings and goings, be nothing Determined thereto by any thing in us, yet are we called to the Excercise of Commanded Duties, as much as if thereby we were Meriting the thing Courted for, and so as to see our Best Performance, but Filthy Raggs I do the rather Urge the Pursuance of this Grace of Patience for this, that I doubt not but the want thereof has been one of the great Sins in our Day; whence have all these Dreadfull Acts of Compliance

flowed

I iowed, but even from this the LORD delayes his coming. &c. O Dreadfull Relation to leave the way of the LORD becaufe he will not Indulge our Humour. fo far as to come at our Nod, I fay then let us Study Faith and Patience in waiting for our Bleffed LORD and Mafter, who as he will come and will not Tarry fo the time of his coming he keeps in his own Bleffed hand (being an Abfolutely free Agent) and well worthy is he to have it fo, upon many confiderations and this amongft the Reft that his Bleffed time is the Beft time, I fay again truft in him, for Sure I am there was never one that through Grace has been Helped fo to do have ever Repented it, neither was there ever any put to Shame that put their truft in him, go through all that are Recorded in Scripture for Trufters in him, and you fhall find them all Harmonioufly joining in this, Surely it is not in Vain to truft in him, for he is indeed a prefent help in time of need, and to confirm the matter yet more Deareft Freinds, give me leave amongft the Reft to put to my Seal and fay, happy, happy, happy that Soul who through Grace is helped to truft him moft, and who will ought but I have good Reafon fo to do, when they confider how in his Holy Providence he not only brought me into the Furnace, but alfo keeped me Wonderfully in it, and alfo in his own due time and way brought me out of it, h s bleffed felf being the great Agent in the whole Work, and indeed I muft tell it to the Commendation of the Freedom of his Grace, that all the time of my Furnace I wanted not (Counting all the fmall and fhort lafting Clouds, though my own Mifcarriage I was into all that time) his Comfortable and Refrefhing prefence for Eight or Nine Hours, Counting all together the greateft Cloud I had all that time, Flowing from my too Eager-Gripping of my Promifed Efcape (of which before) and Limiting my GOD to that in my Eye, which was yet that by which I Efcaped, this I fay lafted longeft and was indeed foreft, but Bleffed be his Holy Name he no fooner let me fee where the Fault lay, but with the Difcovery gave Grace to Amend it, by laying Life and Death in the Ballance, and keeping them ftill in *I quilibrio*, not Daring fo much as by a Raw Wifh to Caft the Scales, then came I to as much Serenity Peace and Satisfaction of Spirit, as any Mortal could be Capable of, and in this Cafe am through Grace Preferved not only till the Perfecting of the Efcape, but even fince for which I defire you may joyn with me in Blefling his ever Bleffed Name, fo alfo in Praying that this our Prefervation may be both for me and the Reft that Efcaped with me a Refervation for our being further Serviceable to our Good GOD in our Stations and Generations, and that we may be helped of him to Spend the Refidue of our Days, in Advancing the Glory of GOD, On carrying of his Works and Edification of h s People, and Conviction, if Poffible, or otherwife the Terror of his and our Proud and Infolent Enemies.

In the laft place, I come to propofe for the object of our fincere and fingle endeavour, that we'll fail effectualy about the preparing of our felves, to meet our Bleffed Lord and Mafter, whither as to his coming for our Delivery in time, or to Judgement in that Great Day, for my own part I am under a ftrong Impreffion of our Bleffed Lords being upon his way, and am not a little perfwaded, that his Sword is already drawen, it's like I may have fome Differing from me here, this I cannot help ; There is another Impreffion, I am now, and have been under for a confiderable time, that his coming (confidered Complexly) fhall be very Terrible. In this I expect, I fhall have very few Godly Differing from me,

I incline

I Incline the rather to Join this twofold Preparation together, that the Duties Incumbent, in Reference to both are one.

The Duty we would propose to our selves herein in General, being to prepare to meet our GOD, of which these we hinted at before, being no small part, we shall for our further clearnefs here, advise the laying aside of several things that may be Impediments in this Work. And First let us lay aside Worldly Mindednefs. Secondly, Carnall Fears. Thirdly, Our own sins, and these sins that easily befetts us. Fourtly, Our Mixing with the people of thefe Abominations, a cafe very Dangerous to be found in, whither either of the ways our Blessed Lord came. Fiftly, Let us lay aside thefe Unchriftian Fires, Satan has Kindled amongft us, whereby (forgetting that Charity, and Brotherly Love, fo much Inculcate by our Blessed Lord and Master) we are rendered mutually uncapable of Edifying one another reproving and Advising one another, as of doing many other Christian Duties Incumbent, that I he not miftaken here, the Lord is my Witnefs, I intend not, that any fhould harden another in a finfull courfe, or that any fhould do any thing, whereby he may become fharer with another in his Sins; And I know, I have Witneffes not a few in thefe Lands, that can bear me Witnefs, I have Guarded againft this, in no fmall meafure, in the Lords ftrength my felf: And whatever Challenges I have either had from within, or from without in this matter, have been rather for too much Keennefs, then too much Slacknefs in this matter, for which in fo far as it has been finfull, I refufe not Satisfaction in time and place convenient. I fay is it not fad, that Satan has gotten fo much Advantage in this matter, that there are very few in the Land, in Capacity to be Affiftant to one another, and all this through Slighting the method prefcribed by our Blessed Lord in his Word, in Reference to Offences, have Men forgotten altogether, that they are in the Body themfelves? Or have thefe perfons who are clear for Separation upon every Account Reckoned, what to Anfwer to our Blessed Lord and Master, whofe Anfwer to that Queftion, how oft fhall I forgive my Brother, till feven times was, I fay not unto you, Seven times but Seventy times Seven times.

And is it not yet fadder, that a Nation folemnly given to God in Covenant, that Party, who in purfuance of thefe Covenants, are defirous to follow the Lord's own way, which all are equally obliged to, and in which while we all walked, there was not wanting much, very much of the Countenance of the Almighty: I fay, is it not fad, that Party fhould not only have the Common Enemy waiting all Opportunities for their overthrow, under which Notion I comprehend that Papiftical Prelatical Party I have been dealing with above; but alfo that of our own Brethren not a few, fhould be pufhing us with Side and Shoulder: and upon the one hand, if we will not remit a little of the Striftnefs of our Obligation to the Almighty, and with them come and go in the matters of God, and forfake *Mofes* his Example, in not quitting a hove; we muft run the hazard of their diffatisfaction. And on the other hand, if we will not yet be more mad than ever *John* of *Leyden* himfelf was, by others of our Brethren muft we be pufht at. I fay, is it not fad, that the Remnant of the poor Church of *Scotland*, fhould be lying in fuch a fad condition, as upon the one hand to be in the hazard of drowning, to on the other of burning? To you then, my Dear Brethren, I addrefs my felf with this Advice, whatever thefe two Extreams do among themfelves, be fure, firft to do nothing that may ftrengthen either. 2dly. To make Confcience of Prayer for both. 3dly. When occasion offers, to intimate your hearty and earnest desire to them, that they would again turn unto the Lord's way, and not any longer either indanger themselves, or wrong the cause of Christ. 4thly. Let your whole complex Carriage towards the Smell of God, and of Tenderness towards both their Souls and Bodies. I dare not advise, to Reason with either, for I have hitherto found, that not only hardning to them, but also indisposing to the Essayer: A better help in this case, I am sure, will be the pursuance of my Sixth Advice, in order to Preparation for our Blessed Lord's coming ; and that is, let one and all of us stir up our Souls, and all that is within us, to wrestle for a speedy coming : I am sure one Sight of his most Amiable Countenance among us, would avail more in these matters, and every thing else that is wrong among us in bulk, than all the feckless Essays we can make ; though it be yet our Duty in our Stations, to use our utmost Endeavours for reclaiming any that go astray. I have been under a necessity to give this hint, neither is there more discovered thereby than the Physicians know already, having hinted so much in their Examination of me.

My Seventh Advice shall be, O study, study a Soul hunger after our Lord and Master, whose compassions could never suffer him yet to tarry long away from any that were at the point of Starving through his Absence. I shall add this Caution here, look that it be Himself principally, if not only you hunger and Thrist after, for though we may indeed have an eye upon the many precious things that attends his coming, yet these, all how precious soever, they bear but the Shell, his Blessed Self being the very Kernell and Soul of the Mercy ; yea it is Himself that makes Mercies such. Now, my Dearest Friends, in the Exercise of these Duties, we have shortly hinted at, both before, and here more particularly upon this head, with what others Our Blessed Lord Himself may artus to, whether immediatly by His Spirit, or by His Servants of the Ministry. I do nothing doubt, but either of these Comings of Our Blessed Lord and Master, shall be rendred the more Refreshfull unto us.

That this may be yet a little more clear, we shall hint at a word in Reference to either. And first. You know that Mercies coming in the Covenant Channel, are the sweetest and most Soul refreshing Mercies ; and as to either, these mercies that come to us in the way of Duty, these being contained in the Covenant, tho' not from any Vertue in themselves, yet by Our Blessed Lord's appointment in the Covenant, and through Vertue transmitted by his Blessed Self to them in the Covenant : I say, Mercies coming that way are twice Mercies, and Our Lord's coming to his in that way, the Mercy is still the more refreshfull, in this Respect, that to that of his coming, which is Mercy, Mercy in it self ; yet to these it is yet more Mercy, as coming to their Distinct Perception in the Covenant Channel ; whereas while coming to others, His coming shall be to such as a Dream, who while they be well wakened, shall be out of case to feel the Sweetness of the Mercy.

Now let me again Obtest you, Dearest Friends, to make Conscience of these Duties, as you have a Respect to the Glory of GOD, the good of his Cause, the good of your of your own Souls, the Conviction (and if not attainable) the Confounding of Enemies: And beside what of Advantages this shall afford you at his comings, with Deliverance in time, which shall yet neither be few nor small, you shall undoubtedly find much Consolation therefrom, at that his great and last coming.

To which this in a word, you have heard before our Blessed Lords coming to Judgement, shall be to the Wicked so very Terrible, that they shall seek all possible means for shuning the appearance, which yet they shall never get done, and though they great and small, shall cry to Hills and Mountains to fall upon them, to cover and hide them from the Face of the Lamb, yet shall all this Crying be in Vain. But to you, to you that are in Covenant with the Almighty, in and through our Blessed Lord, and have been helped with the wise Virgins, *To keep your Lamps Trimmed,* this appearance shall be so far from being a Surprizall that it shall be the most Joyfull Sound ever you heard in your time? O how Soul Refreshing shall it be to you, when at the call of the last Trumpet, you have Raised up your heads, through these Mooles, and having Soul and Body Joyned together again, at the very first Peep, as you look up shall you see the Lamb of GOD Sitting on his Throne, which shall so much take up all your Senses both Internall and Externall Spirituall and Bodily, that you shall not be in hazard of being Frighted, with the Screicks of the Reprobate, and Wicked, but the whole Motions of our Souls shall be. O To be at him, O To be at him, O how Soul Ravishing shall the sight be

And now must we halt here a little till the Elect be gathered together, during which time let us vent our Meditation of the difference that will be betwixt the Elect and Reprobate, the Reprobate saying Oh alace! for ever yonder he is for the dishonour done to whom we could never shed a Tear, the Elect says well's me yonder he is upon the account of the Dishonour done to whom I have had many a sore Heart, and have shed many a Tear. The Reprobate says, Oh! he is yonder whom I could never either Love or Fear. Says the Elect blessed for ever be the sight, yonder he is who helped me both to Love and Fear him, the Reprobate says, Oh! for ever yonder he is whom I could never be perswaded either to believe, or patiently to wait for. Says the Elect, Rejoice O my Soul for ever, yonder he is that helped me by his Spirit, both to trust in and wait for him, the Reprobate says, Oh, and alace! yonder he is towards the Meeting of whom all the Exhortations in time could never move me to make preparation, says the Elect Glory to his Name for ever he is there now, for Meeting of whom he helped me many a day to be Trimming my Lamp. Says the Reprobate Oh and undone for ever, yonder he is whom in his Members I not only persecuted but Murdered many a time. Says the Elect endless blessings on his ever Glorious Face, for whose sake he helped me to suffer Persecution says one, and to be Hanged on a Gibbet, Beheaded or Drowned say others, and so forth of all the rest of the Duties the Elect have been helped to perform, and against the performance whereof the Reprobate have been hardened, or rather have hardened themselves. Now may we suppose the whole Elect to be gathered together, and looking many a greedy look to be at him, then may we suppose our blessed Lord and Master by his Omnipotent Arm halling them all up to him in the Air: O Glorious Meeting! a Meeting without a parting, a Meeting for Joy unexpressible, then shall they be set down on the Right hand to receive their Sentence, as the Reprobate have done already in our Paper, in order of GOD's appointment they shall be last, as you may see in that 25th *Chap.* of *Matth.* out of which we drew their Sentence, and then shall the Sentence of the Elect be pronunced as follows in the 34 *Verse* of the said 25th *Chap.* of *Matth.* *Come ye blessed of my Father, inherit the Kingdom prepared for you from the foundation of the World.*   Now

Having, through Divine Affiftance, brought my Teftimony to this period, it may be fuppofed my Vital Spirits are not a little wearied ; and fure I am I fhall need to ufe no Argument, to perfwade any that know me Well, that I have never in my Lifetime been fo long Serious together, as I have been, fince my Ever Bleffed LORD and Mafter in his Holy Providence brought me under this fo Lovely Chain, Lovely indeed, yet the Sweeteft time ever I had in my Life time, next to that little time of our Efpoufalls for which my Soul fhall Blefs him forever. I fay fince it is fo, I hope none will Offend if for my Recreation I break here a Jeaft or two, in Referrence to which I hope the rather, I have my Bleffed Mafter's Permiffion that therein I intend to do Defpite to, and Spitt in the Faces of a few, fuch as have with moft Violence and Hellifh Boldnefs, not only done Defpite unto the Spirit, but alfo Monftroufly Spitten in the Face of my Bleffed Lord and Mafter : The Nature of my Jefts fhall be fuch, as we call in *Latin, feria mixta jocis*, and in broad *Scots; half Jeft half Earneft*.

And Firft by way of Advertifement, to all who concern themfelves in the Re-formed Churches of thefe Kingdoms, that they ufe their Moyen with thefe mak-ers of Mugs, whether in that place of *Scotland* called *Muir-madzoun*, or any where elfe up and down the Nations that in Imitation of the *Hollanders*, who (that they might in Remeniberance, of the Cruelty of that Monfter for Blood Thirftinefs the Duke of *Alva*, caufed Imprefs his Picture upon the Face of the Brandy Bottles) they would upon all the Mugs they fhall make, after this im-print on the forepart thereof, the Picture of this our Duke of *Alva* (I mean *York*) and upon the back part thereof, the Picture of that Pitifull thing (*Claver Houfe*) and becaufe they muft not want a Chaplain, upon the Bottom of thefe Mugs, let the Picture of that Monfter (the Bifhop of *Edinburgh*) be Impreff-ed to this effect, that all the Carlines in the Country, may have occafion once in the Twenty four Hours, to vent their Difrefpect to thefe Abominable Wretch-es, that fo with their Names, their very Pictures may Stink alfo, and becaufe their Phyfiognomies may by the Spectators be miftaken, I would advife their feveral Names might be Adjoined to their Pictures, leaft they looking to *Yorks* Picture, might take it for that of a Serpent, or to *Claver Houfe* his Picture for that of a Snake, or that Monfter the Bifhop of *Edinburgh* his Picture, for that of a Meer Swine Wallowing in Filth. Yet I will not be Peremptor here, for the miftake will not be great in any of thefe ; And now having mett with the Bifhop, that you may fee I wrong him not, be pleafed to take a glance of him in thefe particulars following: And firft, In a Dialogue betwixt him and that prodigious Drunkard, Mr. *Trotter* one of his Underlings (even that *Trotter*, who (it would appear) having anticipated the Dyet of drinking our Dragie, had got himfelf fo full, that Morning our bleffed Lord fet us at liberty , that he took Stowre for Spicak

ncings of his own firie eyes for Light Matches, which occasioned
erting of the Pulpit, (a place he never deserved to set his foot in)
fusion of his Auditors as follows, Having met together Oc-
op says to Trotter, How now Mr. Trotter, I am informed you are
ard Mr. Trotter ? My Lord, do you Believe that ? Bishop Yes
all Men says so. Trotter I am very sorry for that my Lord, for
u are a Scandalous Adulterer, yet I do not believe it Bishop say
s Bishop Then to be quits with You neither will I believe the
1ay inform your selves of the Nature and qualities of that his
I am informed is in the Hands of Sir Charles Halket, which I
Generous Gentleman keeps for no other end but to be a Witness
the abominable Madness of that Mock Prophet, one of whose
to offer to your Confideration, in the third place as follows,
Hehill of Edinburgh in Company of the Duke of York and others,
1680, or beginning of 1681, looking to that great Comet that
d being asked by the Duke What his Thoughts of the Comet were ?
tpon it as a Torch in the Heavens to light your Royal Highness
this Prodigious Monster know what he was saying, when he
10t know the many standing Laws of this Kingdom, were Bars
vhich are yet standing, and still shall stand ? I mean these men
apists having any Place of Publick Trust in the Nation. Does
w, that thir Laws are standing and must stand, being found-
e to the Word of GOD, and enacted by free Parliaments ?
1te Wretch know, that any Act made to the contrary can ne-
of Laws in this Nation, as being down right contrary to the
enacted by untree Parliaments ? Must we weary our selves
n and again ? And did not this Monster for arrogant Boldness,
10w that by the Word of GOD our Supream Law it is enacted
I die the Death ? Or is he so wretchedly blind as not to know
t, that Man of sin and all his Limbs (of which this Duke of his
are Idolaters ?) What could possess this Infatuate Wretch
iis Mock Prophesie, Sure nothing but the Devil) it is like that
1 Lying Spirit in the Mouth of Ahab's Prophets, of which you
I Chapter of the first Book of the Kings from the 20 Verse to the
1 I be neither a Prophet, nor the Son of a Prophet (as all who
et may I not venture to Vent a few of my Guesses in this mat-
vs but I may hit nearer the Truth than this Mock and Madly

this Comet was designed a Torch (if he will have it so,) for
way into Germany, whom our Blessed LORD may make use of
and their Neighbouring Nations, and by whom our Glorious
1g inquiry for the Blood lying in the Streets of the great ones;
y House of Austria. Secondly, What if it were lighting in
the head of his Hungarian Forces, to prove the Lawfullness of
1g thereto Necessitate by the Violence they met with from that
Jesuites, both as to their Civils and Spirituals ? Thirdly,
ht to the Protestants in France, Britain, Ireland and elsewhere,
; of the Mists cast upon that Scripture, Sell they Coat and Buy a

G   Sword

Sword, by the *Jesuitiesd* Parties at Home and Abroad, Rolled
What if this great Comet, was sent as a Warning of the *Fall of*
of Sin, and all who have sent their strength to that *Whore*, and
Combined against the LORD, and *against his Anointed*, and to U
on of *Rome*, as another not much unlike it, did that of *Jerusa*
hopefull, that these my Guesses shall hold much better, then in
Daring Prophesie, of that Abominable Letcherous Wretch Bish
in him have we two Old *Scots* Proverbs made good: First,
first in the Mire. Secondly, *Patersons Mare goes foremost*.

My second Jest shall be this, I am apprehensive some may be
it shall befall me as it did that Man, *Who for telling the Truth, c*
any where. This Man being wandering towards the Evening,
(I will not say it was our Chancelor, but I think it was one like I
How now Friend, what do you Travelling so late? The other
Lodging. Go with me Friend, says the other : So they came he
set down, when the Poor Traveller being Dry, calls to his L
end me the Cup by you? Upon which he takes his Batton; and
o the Door, under Cloud of Night. And indeed our Chancelc
Unchristian and madly wicked, what could move the Man's Sp
sure I am, (whatever I thought, yet) I call'd him not *Gleid C*
raised his Passion, that I told him he had sworn in the *Test*; Th
cy, *as explain'd, was horrid Blasphemy*. And was not this
Principles and Practices I there owned? And did I not offer fi
to Vindicate this? Why am I then, by Armed Force, halled
other? (In this he was worse than the other Gleid Carl, wh
tho' he would not give him Lodging) And there I must be ar
stices (who to compliment the Chancelor) (or may be the I
the World see, that they are as gleid in their Morals, as the oth
by them forsooth, tho offering Vindication from GOD's Wor
be granted, that the Almighty is Supream Judge, and his W
I am (upon the matter) denyed both, (as you may see befor
on an Assize, who outdoing both, did shew themselves stone
Pannal off their hands on these Terms : But for this, as for w
these Lands of this Nature, are these horrid Monsters, foi
Blessed Lord in his Members, to Answer before Our Ever Ble
my Instrument standing upon Record in Heaven, at that grea
say, Some may be under this Impression anent me, but I shall
pect shelter, even the LORD; for, *The Name of the Lord*
righteous flee thereunto, and are safe. As also, in that Script
and Mother forsake me, the Lord will take me up. This has o
me, and so long as I have a BIBLE, containing these and many
prehensions of the former shall never much trouble me.

I remember in the former part of my Testimony, I Advised
to burden themselves with my Blood; and the Blood of these
with me, as much as if they had gotten their unparalelled cru
cution, I give here the Reason, even because of the Keenness t
after us after our escape, which I look upon as a fighting again
of GOD, and a fretting at his Holy Dispensations, and in this

Rage ran that height, that not having anew of two footed, they make use of Four footed Dogs to Sent us out. It's like they be yet ignorant of the Reason why these Dogs could not find us, therefore I shall lend them even this, there was no Blood hanging at our heels, and I hope, yea, and trusts very firmly, that turn the Chase when it will, which I yet hope shall be sooner than either his Peoples fainting fears, or his and our Enemies groundless hopes will allow either to believe. I say, come that Day when it will, I hope the Lord's People shall be at this Advantage in finding of them to be brought to Judgement, that the feckleseft Curr in the Country that has the least of the Sent of Blood, shall never miss one of them, since upon every individual (as we told you before) is there no less Blood lying, *than all the Righteous Blood shed from Righteous Abel,* till this Hour. *Now most Glorious and Infinitely Blessed LORD GOD, even haften thy coming; as for the Comfort af the weary Mourners, so for the Terrour and Confusion of these Builders of Babel, thine. and ours for thy sake cruel and Bloody Enemies.* Thus very Cordially Prays, JOHN DICK.

A Brief Account of what passed betwixt the Council and Mr. John Dick *upon the Fourth Day of* March 1684, *being the Day before he Suffered.*

MR. *John Dick,* who was Inftrumental of and Acceffary to, your Efcaping out of Prifon? Where have you Haunted, and with whom have ye Frequented, fince that time? My Lords, *if ye had no other to Enquire at then me, ye might have caufed take me from the Court of Guard to the Gibbet.* Do ye own and adhere to all your former Actings? *I both own and adhere to all that I have done in the Vindication of my Principles, and in the Reproving, if not the Converting of Chrifts Enemies, either with my Tongue or Pen, and am willing to Seal the fame with my Dearest Blood.*

Follows an Account of what passed betwixt the Lords of Justiciary, and Mr. John Dick, *when his Sentence was reintimate to him, the next Day after he was taken.*

THE Lords hearing of it, being Conveened he was brought from the Tolbooth, and put in the Pannel before them, to whom he gave a Bow, and fo the Clerk at the Command of the Lords Cryed to the Macer faying, Macer Command Silence, then they called Mr. *John Dick,* to whom he Anfwered here I am, and fo the Clerk Read as follows. *Mr.* John Dick *now ftanding in the Pannel, having been apprehended before to wit in* Auguft laft, *and having been feveral times before the Lords of Council and Jufticiary, was Sentenced, and Commanded upon the fifth Day of* September 1683, *to be Hanged at the* Grafs Mercat *of* Edinburgh *upon the 26th. of of that inftant, but the faid Mr.* John Dick *having Broken the Toolbooth of this Brugh upon the 16th. of that inftant, and feveral others with him, and fo made his Efcape before the time that he fhould have been Hanged, and we, being apprehended and now ftanding in the Pannel thefe are to Warrand, Authorize, Command and Charge the Magiftrates of this Burgh, to Caufe Carefuly Conduct him to the faid* Grafs-Mercat *of* Edinburgh *to Morrow, between two and four in the Afternoon, and there to be Hang'd up till he be Dead, under the pain of the Act. &c.*

At the hearing of which, he gave a Bow to the Lords and faid, now my Lords, the Sentence that your Lordships paffed upon me both before and now, is both unreafonable and unjuft, and contrar to the Laws of this Nation; however, it is very welcome to me upon Chrift's Account. But I remember two things that I demanded before, and now I demand them again. The firft was, That the great *Jehovah* is Judge of Heaven and Earth, and that all the Kings and Princes therein are but his Deputes and Servants, this was granted me before. The Second was, That the Scriptures are the Supream Law, and that all the Laws of this Nation and all other Nations are to be regulate thereby, and strike and Vail their Capes to this, this they refused me before, and now I demand it again, but he got no Answer: So he cryed, now my Lords, I take the Great GOD to Witness, and each of your Consciences to Witness against your selves, and all of you, and the rest of this multitude to Witness against you that hears me, that ye have again refused me this to grant it to me, and tho ye have judged me once before and now again unjustly: Yet remember, that at one Day GOD will Judge you, and Reviving my Blood, and the Blood of all my Brethren that has been shed unjustly, and they cryed that they would take him away and not suffer him to speak any longer, so he rapped upon the Breast of the Pannel and cryed out, (GOD even my GOD) shall Judge you as ye have Judged me, and that ye shall find, but GOD forgive you, and I forgive you, if it be agreeable to his Eternal Decree, and so he was taken away, crying as he went to the Door of the Outter House, saying, well I am refused of that which none but Heathens could have refused me of, but I bliss the LORD for it, and many of my Christian Friends knows my Mind of these things, and others may know it when I am gone.

Followes his Words and Carraige in the Laigh Council House, that Afternoon he came from the Tolbooth, before he went to the Scaffold, as I was there, present, after the Reading of the Sentence, Mr. Ramsay one of the Ministers of the Old Kirk of *Edinburgh*, offered to Pray to him, to whom he Replyed. Sir how dare you presume, or how dare you have the Confidence to pray in my Presence, since ye are Fighting against GOD, and Persecuting Christ in his Members ye have not only Abjured the Covenant, but is Murdering the Souls of the LORD's people, and to Crown all your Abjured ones, and Abominations: Have he not taken that Abominable *Test.* Mr. *Ramsay.* Answers, Well Sir, will ye pray your self then, Yes if the Bailie suffer me I will, if ye will promise to make no Reflections in Prayer; But he Answered, that he would make no such promises; But said he, whatsoever GOD gives me to pray, that will I pray. And so the Baillie again, Refused to suffer him, if he would not promise, not to have any Reflections in Prayer, but he Answered as before; But Mr. *Ramsay* pressed the Baillie to give him Liberty to pray, and he began to pray thus. (O Lord God, the Great God, and my Covenanted God, and the Covenanted God of Scotland; For Christs Sake, come with Deliverance to thy Church and People, and help them, Vindicate and make great thy Glory. And so the Bailie cryed to take him away.

The last Words and Carriage of Mr. John Dick, who Suffered in the Grass Market of Edinburgh, upon the Fifth of March 1684.

WHen he went upon the Scaffold, he Beckned to the Multitude, beginning at North side thereof, and so turning himself Round with a Smiling Countenance, and no less Couragious then pleasant Demonstrations, without the least of Terrour, or being Troubled, either with Death near approaching, or the manner of the Death he was to Die, this in a Princely like Posture, he presented himself in the fight of all there present; And then with his hands Falded together, and his Eyes lifted up to Heaven for a little, looking not only stedfastly but Eagerly, and so Streaching furth his hands, he began thus.

The

(53)

The great Confluence that are gathered together here, manifestly declares to me, that many if not the great part of this Multitude expects and looks for some thing more than Ordinary, but ye may be disappointed, I nothing doubt but all of this Multitude, at least the most part knows and have heard that I have had near six Months Respite more than was allowed me by Men, which time was granted me in the Goodness and Mercy of GOD through my Escape, which Mercy I mean this time that I have had since my escape, I look upon it to have been given me for these two, and in both these that GOD may be Glorified. And First, That having so much more time, I might have the Liberty and Priviledge more fully to exhibite and give in my Judgment; At which Bailie *Chanceller* called to Beat, but he stops him saying, Beat not, and so he proceeded saying, Secondly, That having so much more time I might the better make ready, and prepare my self for that great Work I have now in hand, I mean Death and Eternity, neither of which is terrifying nor dumping to me, for the which and all other of his Favours and Mercies which he in the abundance of his Goodness, and Riches of his free Grace bestowed on me, even one me who while in a Natural State was as evil and abominable in Gods sight as any here at this time: I desire to bless, Adore, Admire, Exalt, and praile the Lord, while in time; for I know I shall shortly praise him without Interruption or Intermiffion; I say it again, I bless him for all his Mercies and Favours conferred upon me, and not only this among the rest, but above all next to that great one, that he made me his own by his Purchase and so became mine, and altho' I have not keeped all right as to him, yet he has keeped all right as to me and betwixt him and me all is right, his other Mercies and Favours that he has condescended so much to Dignifie and Honour me, as to Crown all in me with Martyrdom.

At which the Bailie called again Beat, but he stoped him saying, ye need not Beat, for ye shall have no Cause of Beating, so he Cryed out saying: Now my Dear Freinds in Christ, it is your Affiftance I Crave in this Exercife of Praifing, let me Befeech you to join with me in Singing to the Praise of this, *even my GOD and the GOD of my Confolation and Salvation, I fay to the Father Son and Holy Ghost, let us Sing Praife from the beginning of the 2d. Pfalm:* So having Sung that Pfalm through which we Sang with great Chearfulness, and fometimes Pointing with his Hands to one Art and fometimes to another, but Especially when he Sang the 6th 7th and 8th. Verfes, his Countenance fo Shined, that it might eafily appeared, to Judicious and Pious Spectators, that he was in an Excelent Frame, and in a Special way to be Helped, to Sing Praife to the LORD, and having done with Singing, he faid with a Pleafent Countenance, I nothing doubt but amongft this great Confluence of People, there are many that are nearer and Dearer to our Exalted and Glorified Lord Jefus Chrift, therefore I shall Addrefs my felf to two Sorts, and shall Speak a short Word to each of thefe as Providence and time shall allow me, firft I shall Speak to Friends, Secondly to Enemies, at which the Bailie called to Beat, but he stopped him saying, forbear Beat not, for ye have had no Cause to Beat as yet, neither shall ye have any Caufe hereafter, and fo he Proceeded faying, as to you that are Freinds, I mean all fuch as are Refolved to follow our Blefled LORD fully through Good Report and Bad Report Coft what it will, I fay according to the Rule that he hath given in his Word.

I fay I have three words of good News to tell you, and as the Words of a Dying Man. And Firft it shall be well with the Righteous, yea verily it shall be well with the Righteous. Now in speaking to this, I would fay two things, but do not

miftake

miſtake me; For I am neither a Miniſter nor a Preacher, for I am not going to preach, but only to give my laſt Advice to theſe here, which I ſhall do in a few words; For neither do I deſire to weary yon, nor to ſpeak, much more the Body being ſhortly to be caught up above the Clouds, pointing with his hand up to Heaven, I mean my Soul, which ſhall be immediatly there. And Firſt, That you my Friends may underſtand me, that the Righteouſneſs of none can make you Righteous but Chriſt, and he Imputed to you for Righteouſneſs: So I ſay, ye moſt have a Borrowed Righteouſneſs, even the Righteouſneſs of Jeſus Chriſt imputed to you, and this is the way that ye moſt be Righteous, I ſay it ſhall be well with the Righteous, the Spirit of GOD, hath ſaid it in his word, and that is better than an Angel had ſpoken it from Heaven, for we have a more ſure word of Propheſie, 2 *Peter* 1 Chap. and 16 Verſe, at which the Bailie ſaid, what Sir are ye going to Preach to whom he Anſwered, yet Smiling, I am not Preaching, but leaving my laſt Advice to theſe here, as not only I am, but as others are Engaged to GOD, that I ſhould Admoniſh my Chriſtian Friends and Acquaintances in Chriſt, while I am in the Body; And now this being my laſt Appearance for GOD, I am bound thereto; Therefore I intreat you, Yea I Charge, that ye would not Interrupt me, and ye ſhall have no cauſe to Beat Drums, and ſo he proceeded ſaying. But Secondly to be Righteous, is not to ſit down, nor reſt Satisfied, with what ye have attained, but to preſs foreward to the Prize, and ſo walking Anſwerable to what ye have Received, and to what ye profeſs, not being Satisfied with what ye are or may appear, to be in the Eyes of Men, but ſtudy a holy and inward way, and walking in the ſight of GOD, and all Men, that ye are the perſons that have this imputed Righteouſneſs imputed to you, and ſo labour to have your Light ſo to ſhine before Men, that ye may Glorifie your Heavenly Father, and ſuch as are theſe Righteous, I ſay it ſhall be well with them.

Then a Second word of good News I have to tell you my Friends is this, that Jeſus Chriſt is ſitting at the Helm of Affairs, and whatever he will he doth it, and there is none that is able to ſtop him when he worketh, and whatſoever his pleaſure is, cometh to paſs, this man thinketh he is working one peice of Work, and a Second Man thinketh he is working an other peice of Work, and a Third Man thinketh he is working his peice of Work, and it may be all are working contrar one to another as they think, and yet for all that they are all working and carrying on his work even when they think they are doing that which at leaſt ſome of them would have done the quite contrary; ſo I ſay in all theſe, they are all working and carying on Chriſt's work. Now my Friends, I exhort all of you, yea, I obteſt you for Chriſt's ſake weary not of GOD, but wait on him and keep his way, I mean, the way appointed in His Word, and truſt him with his own work, for all that has been done, or ſhall ever be done by the Actions of Men to the contrar, yet his work is ſtill carried on thereby; ſo Leppen to GOD and ye ſhall not be diſappointed. But a Third word of Good News that I have to tell you is this, that notwithſtanding of all the dark Clouds that has been and now are, yet I can aſſure you, that there are Glorious Days coming, to this Covenanted Lands, and I aſſure you, yea, I dare aver it, that they are ✴ reer than ye at leaſt a great part even of the Godly that are does believe, I ſay it again, Sirs there are Glorious Days coming to this Lands, & even to poor and filthy Carlives, and I am certain ſhe is both poor and filthy enough, ye and ſhe are very near to one another, therefore I entreat you beware of Misbelief and Impatience; and ye would not keep back theſe Days, beware of Sin that may procure the ſame. So now my Friends, I have theſe few Advices to leave with you, and firſt, I requeſt you, labour to make your foundation sure and Right, I say before ye ingage in a Profession.

I entreat you as a Dying Man, and take it amongst my Last Words; Lay a Foundation sure, for without this ye will never be able to do or suffer aright for Christ, when it comes to this with it, either Sin or Suffer: I say, ye will never be able to suffer acceptably, if ye have not the Foundation laid sure. Will ye know why it is and from whence it flows, that so many have made shipwreck of GOD, CHRIST, and a good Conscience, in a Day of Tryal; and why so many have broken down that which once they builded, or at least seemed to be Builders of, and are denying that which once they professed, and fighting against that which once they fought with and for, and so are fled from their Ground: Here is the Reason, because they stood and Built upon a Sandy Foundation; therefore lay the Foundation sure and right, if ye will stand it out in a Day of Tryal: And that this may be thereby considered, remember Sirs, ye may meet with harder Tryals than this is, that I am meeting with, I mean in your Eyes, for it is not sharp to me; yea the Thoughts and fearfull Apprehensions of what Tryals others may meet with that I have, makes me so much the more to be satisfied, and to rejoice in my Lot. But I say it again, Sirs, Lay the Foundation right, and ye that will not lay it, nor make it your Study to have it laid right; I say to you, wait with your perfection, and profess nothing but what you practise.

My Second-Advise to you is this, that having laid the Foundation Sure and Right, ye would be still Building and Carrying on Chrifts Work, untill it be Perfited, I mean till your Conversation in all things be Suitable to the Gospel, and Answerable to that Foundation Built up and Rooted in your most Holy Faith, & in all your Building, let Faith Patience and all other of the Graces be lively in Exercise, that so your Building may go Right on.

My Third Advise to you my Freinds is this, Labour to Love one another, I say to all the People of GOD here and else where, Love one another, yea, Labour to Love one another more and more, and to bear with one another, and Beware of needless and Groundless Sinfull Breaking and Divisions, I do not say that ye will joyn with any in Sin and Combine against GOD and his Christ in Sinfull ways and Courses, but Labour to bear with one another and Strengthen, Edify, Exhort, Confirm and Comfort one another, and this is the way to gain one another, and I am Perswaded that the needless, Groundless and Sinful Division, and Breakings that have been in the Land, have more wronged the Cause, Interest, Work and Peolpe of GOD, then all the Devils and Men could have done, and has not the Devil had a Speciall Hand in the Breakings and Divisions of the LORD's People, that thereby he might Rout the same, therefore in Consideration and Commemoration of these things, study unity and Honesty in the LORD, at which the Bailie

what ye now poſſeſs, I ſay it again, improve what Mercies a
and labour to improve every opportunity, either of doing or
ber that time is precious, and ye muſt give an account how
all other Mercies that ye enjoy.

My firſt Advice to you is, labour to be of a Sympathizei
concerned with the Glory of GOD, and with a Suffering C
and do not think you Sympathize with him and yet be unconc
Chriſts Members; for a Sympathizeing with them ſhall be lo
him as a Concernedneſs with and in him, and what ye do
them it ſhall be Rewarded by him, as if ye had done it to or
and ſo walk in this and all other Duties ſutable to your bei
Friends my laſt Advice to you is this, Labour, O labour to
Sincerity in all theſe and other Duties, and ſo ye ſhall have Pe
and now my Friends that ye and all the People of GOD may l
us Pray to GOD, even my GOD) yea I ſay it without Vanity
ſo to him let us Pray. Not being Permitted to Speak to the Sec
Enemies, and after he Prayed, he Read the Ninth Chapter of
now and then looking up to the Windows on both ſides, b
North ſide, where he Eſpyed many eſt-Faces that he knew, m
with his Hands and Eyes, as he Read, to the Perſons to whom t
moſt to be applyed, and then he Sang a part of the Thirty Seve
Twenty Ninth Verſe: So having Prayed, there was one Paſſ
beyond the Reſt, which was this (O LORD ſince thou haſt F
here, to lay down my Life for thy Cauſe and Intereſt, I Pray e
up this Ladder with me, and to Lead me through the Dark
of Death, that is Us known to all Naturely, and I know that
Soul in the down coming thereof, after that he call's fo
which was Immediatly brought unto him, and he taking it i
morePleaſent Countenance then he ſeemed to have before, ſays
winn foreward, Pointing with his Hand to the Ladder, th
Captain Graham, he ſaid to him Sir do me the Favour to call i
and ſaid Suffer him to come up to me upon the Scaffold,
him, ſo Deſireing ſuch as were not Concerned might be put d
then he with a Smilling Countenance turns to the People, ar
Cowngie as he did when he went firſt up the Scaffold, and tu
was alſo upon the Scaffold with him, and Embracing him very
ſeveral Kiſſes, and Rounded ſome of his laſt Adviſes to him, an
ſaying, (LORD be with you my Dear Father.)

And then turned to his Brother, who was alſo by him upon t
the ſame manner Embracing him & Kiſſing, & ſo parted with hir
ſame purpoſe that he had to his Father, with an Exhortation, that
Life, and forbear his Idle Company; But eſpecially his ways v
that Nature, ſelling him the Hazard thereof, and encouragi
follow his laſt Advices; Then he turns to two Gentlemen w
him, and after the ſame manner Embraced, Saluted and par
then he gave another Bow to the whole Multitude, and ſo w
and turning his Face to the North-Eaſt, he Cryed out, ſaying,
day to lay down my Life, which I do willingly and Chearſu

surprised nor terrified with Death or the manner of it: And here I do declare I would not Exchange my Lot with what the greatest King, Prince, or Emperors Enjoyments could afford me, and what I Speak once I say it again, I lay down my Life willingly and Chearfully for Christ and his truth, Blessing him that ever I had a Life to lay it down for him, yea I am now no more Troubled with or for Death, then if I were to ly down in the Finest Bed that the Earth could afford, with the most Dear and Intimate Friend that the World could allow me, and here I do Declare, that I do Heartily and freely forgive all Men, whatsoever they have done to or against me, and Prayes that the LORD would forgive them, I forgive them that sentenced me to die here, first and last; and I forgive all that apprehended me first and last, or was any way accessory thereto; and I forgive all that has brought me here, and are guarding me here; and I forgive this Poor Man, pointing with his hand behind him to the Hangman, who is to be my Executioner. Now I desire you all, especially you who pretend to be righteous, Study to be Sincere in the Way of GOD, and in working out of your Salvation; for there are many who pretends to be Godly, that know little of the Life and Power thereof: therefore I entreat you labour to know what is the Power and Life of Godliness; for there are many, if not the most part, who pretends to be righteous, that knows least of it. I say, be not satisfied with the Shell, but labour for the Kernel and Marrow of Religion. Now, my Friends, Remember I tell you here upon the Ladder, and as a Dying Man stepping out of Time to Eternity, that notwithstanding all the Dark Clouds that has been, and now are, yet there are a thicker and darker coming, and it is not far off, yea it is at hand. But I say, Trust in GOD, Trust in GOD and he will not disappoint you, I say Trust in GOD whatever Afflictions befall you, yet Trust in GOD and give him Credite. At the hearing of these Words the Bailie calls to Beat the Drums, and so they were Beat a little, at which he looked down to the Bailie and said, what Sir do ye Beat Drums; because I desire the People to trust in GOD? and the Drums were silenced, Then he Cryed out again trust in GOD, and ye shall be born through, if once ye get in him and keep in him. Then he said I will Sing a part of the twenty fifth *Psalm* from the sixteen *Verse* to the close, for it has been many a time very sweet to me, and so I will sing it as my last Song in Time, I shall be immediatly where my Heart shall be so Tuned, pointing with his Hand to his Breast, that I shall never be able to stop the Melody and Harmony thereof, then having Sung these *Verses* he Prayed, in which among other things he had this Expression, *Lord take a Course with thine Enemies, and these of them whom thou has a Purpose of Love to, Lord bring them in and let them see the evil of their ways, and these that are thine incorrigible Enemies make the Wheels of thy Chariots go over their Backs: And now Lord leave me not, and leave not thine to the evil of the Enemies, hasten*

and it being Tyed, and his Brother offering to pull it over his Face he (putting away his Hand with his) said let alone, I will draw it down my self, so he puts his Hands into his Pocket, and takes out the Cover of his Bible, and putting the same therein he gave it to his Brother, Charging him straitly to give it to his Sister. Then he looked round about him, saying farewell all my Friends in CHRIST pointing with his Hand to some that he knew, both in Windows and on the Street to one (fixing his Eyes upon him) he said my Dear Billie the Lord be with you, the Lord be with you, and having fixed himself upon a Step of the Ladder said.

I Remember a Passage of *Abraham*, who was Commanded to Sacrifice his Son *Isaac*, he having in Obedience to the Command brought his Son to offer him up a Sacrifice; Reared up an Altar, and *Isaac* says to him here is the Altar and there is the Wood, but where is the Sacrifice and then he said (Pointing to the Gibbet) here is the Altar, and then Pointing to the Ladder on which he Sat, said here is the Wood and then he said (laying his Hands on his Breast) and Blessed be GOD here is a free will offering, and I will give it willingly and Chearfuly, yea I can say it, here even upon the Brink of Eternity, that these several Years I have Preferred the Glory of GOD, the wellfare and Prosperity of the Work and Interest of Christ and his People; to my own Private and Particular Interest, and I might have Shunned such a Death as this, but GOD knows I durst not do it.

And now, I know, yea I am firmly perswaded, That my Dear Lord even my Exalted and Glorified Lord Jesus Christ, will carry me safely throw this Dark Valley and Saddow of Death, and will receive my Soul immedatly after I go off this Ladder unto Glory, where I shall ever be with him. Then he said again (crying with a Loud Voice) now when I can Hardly get Speaking for the Rope about my Neck Farewell all Freinds and followers of Christ, & again I say Farewell, and Adiew all Earthly Enjoyments, and so (having given the Hangman a Sign when he would be ready) he Prayed alitle within himself, and when he had done, he gave the Sign and at the giving thereof he drew the Napkin over his Face, and Cryed out, Farewell all Friends in Christ, & into thy Hands O Lord do I Commit my Soul. So he was Turned over. And so ends the Life of this Faithful and now Glorified Martyr for Christ, And to GOD the Father Son and Bessed Spirit, be Eternal Praise and Glory for ever and ever Amen.

F I N I S.

www.ingramcontent.com/pod-product-compliance
Lightning Source LLC
Chambersburg PA
CBHW031750090426
42739CB00008B/949